I0559163

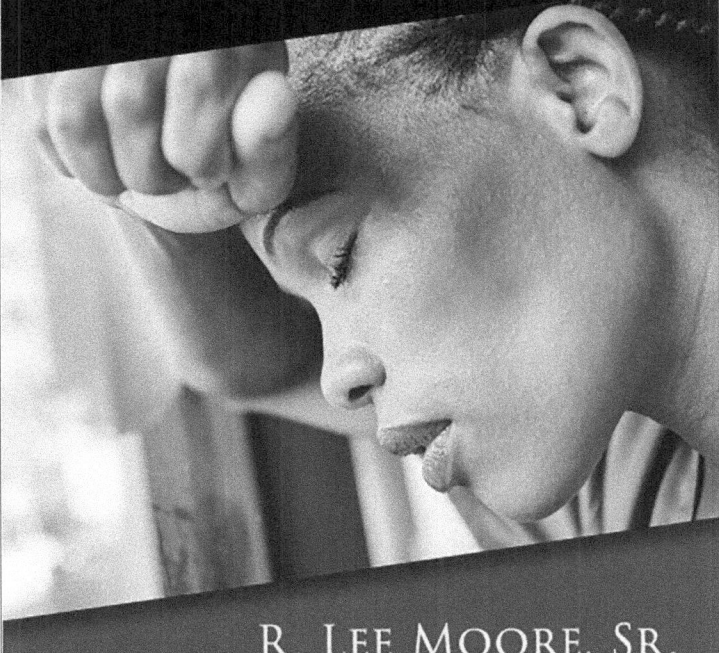

A CAREGIVER'S CALL FOR HELP

Why Won't They
JUST DIE...

R. LEE MOORE, SR.

Copyright © 2024 by Ronald L. Moore, Sr.
WHY WON'T THEY JUST DIE

Printed in the United States of America

All rights reserved under the United States Copyright Act
of 1976. Contents may not be reproduced in whole or in part
in any form without express written consent of the author.

Cover design and book layout;
All graphics designed by
R. Lee Moore, Sr.

One Creative Mind, LLC
ISBN: 979-8-9905229-0-9 SOFT COVER
ISBN: 979-8-9905229-1-6 EBOOK

"THERE ARE ONLY FOUR KINDS OF PEOPLE
IN THE WORLD,

THOSE WHO HAVE BEEN CAREGIVERS.

THOSE WHO ARE CURRENTLY CAREGIVERS.

THOSE WHO WILL BE CAREGIVERS,
AND THOSE WHO WILL NEED A CAREGIVER."

— Rosalynn Carter

DEDICATED TO THOSE
WHO HAVE SACRIFICIALLY
GIVEN CARE TO OTHERS.

Contents

Introduction

When a caregiver experiences the thought, but refrains from voicing it, "why won't they just die!" they are not actually expressing a wish for the death of their loved one.

Rather, this expression is a way of venting their frustration and feelings of helplessness.

Caregivers provide care out of love and obligation, but it can be exhausting, especially when the recipient's needs are demanding.

As a full-time caregiver, I never thought how enormous the task would be. I believed I could handle whatever came my way. After all, caregiving is merely watching over someone you know and love; making sure they are safe and comfortable. Boy, was I wrong! The truth is, the invisible emotional toll it takes becomes very visible in time. It is often too much to bear.

That's why I wrote the book, *"Why Won't They Just Die!"*

It's important to understand the context in which caregivers use this expression. It's often used in a moment of overwhelm, a time when the caregiver feels that they've reached their limit.

It's also often expressed out of a sense of desperation, a situation where they feel like they're running out of options.

Caregivers are ordinary people who take on an extraordinary responsibility. They provide care and support to family members who are aging, ill, or disabled. Caregiving is a very demanding job, and caregivers may experience physical and emotional stress, financial struggles, and other difficult situations. Misconceptions about the role of caregiving make it difficult for those who provide care, as well as for the recipient.

"CAREGIVING IS A CHALLENGING JOB"

The good news, however, is that we don't have to go through this dark tunnel alone. In my book, I share stories of encouragement and instruction of how to recognize and manage these emotions. I offer solutions to help caregivers find the support they need and how to take care of themselves, too. Simply put, we can't take care of others if we're not taking care of ourselves first.

One of the most beneficial and intriguing features of this "info-novel" are the stories depicting caregivers' experiences. I can relate to many of them shared letting me know I am not alone. We need to be encouraged to see the brightly shining light at the end of the tunnel, the moments of joy and love that make it all worthwhile. And we need to acknowledge the moments of frustration and anger, the times when we feel like giving up, so that we can find ways to move past them.

A Caregiver Defined

A caregiver or carer is a paid or unpaid member of a person's social network who helps them with activities of daily living. Since they have no specific professional training, they are often described as informal caregivers. Caregivers most commonly assist with impairments related to old age, disability, a disease, or a mental disorder.

Typical duties of a caregiver might include taking care of someone who has a chronic illness or disease; managing medications or talking to doctors and nurses on someone's behalf; helping to bathe or dress someone who is frail or disabled; or taking care of household chores, meals, or processes both formal and informal documentation related to health for someone who cannot do these things alone.

With an aging population in all developed societies, the role of caregiver has been increasingly recognized as an important one, both functionally and economically. Many organizations that provide support for persons with disabilities have developed various forms of support for carers as well.

A Caregiver's Passion

"What I love about being a caregiver is the ability to

make a positive impact on people's lives," said Victoria.

Victoria always knew that caregiving was her calling. As a little girl, she was known for her nurturing and caring personality. She used to take care of her siblings, and they always felt well taken care of by her. Victoria felt that she could use her strengths to make a positive impact on people's lives, and caregiving would allow her to do so.

Victoria's journey to becoming a caregiver began with taking classes and earning certifications. She learned the importance of empathy, communication, and patience when working with patients. She understood that caregiving required more than just professional knowledge and certification. It required a warm and compassionate nature that comes naturally to her.

"EMOTIONAL TURMOIL OF CAREGIVERS OFTEN GO UNNOTICED"

Victoria added that "I have a genuine passion for caregiving, and I believe that my patients need that kind of passion from me. It's about more than just providing care - it's about making a difference and improving the quality of someone's life."

Victoria landed her dream job at a local nursing home where she worked with elderly patients who needed assistance with everyday tasks. Her colleagues and patients quickly recognized her for her kind and compassionate nature. Victoria made sure to spend enough time with each patient, listening to their stories, and sharing in their joys and sorrows. She believed in treating every patient with respect, dignity, and kindness.

In Victoria's own words, "Being a caregiver is not just about providing care but also about forming connections. I believe that every patient deserves my full attention and care."

As the years went by, Victoria formed deep connections with many of her patients. She learned about their lives and listened to their stories. Her patients shared their sorrows and joys with her, and Victoria always tried to give them a sense of comfort and support.

"If you show genuine compassion for your patients, you get to understand more about their lives and what they have gone through. You get to create a bond that makes you more like a friend than just a caregiver," added Victoria.

Victoria's reputation as a caregiver quickly spread among families who needed someone to care for their loved ones. She became recognized by her colleagues and seniors for her outstanding work.

Victoria's nursing supervisor shared, "Victoria is a great member of our team. She always goes above and beyond to make sure her patients are happy and comfortable, and we couldn't ask for more from her."

Although Victoria has retired, her legacy as a caregiver lives on. Her patients remember her kindness and compassion, and the families she served are grateful for the care she provided to their loved ones.

As Victoria said, "I am proud of my work as a caregiver. I believe that being compassionate and caring is something that can stay with someone for their entire life."

In the end, Victoria's story is a testament to the power of caregiving and the impact one person can have on the lives of many. Her passion, kindness, and compassion made her a great caregiver, and her legacy will live on in the people whose lives she touched.

Why Won't They Just Die! An overview...

As a full-time caregiver, you offer a remarkable level of dedication, compassion, and care to your loved one. However, this selfless act can often come at a cost to your mental, physical, and emotional health. In this info novel, we aim to uncover the hidden emotions of full-time caregivers, with a focus on understanding the pain points and providing solutions. We offer stories that bring the issues to the forefront using real life examples. Throughout this book, we delve into the heart of the matter, exploring the emotional turmoil that can often go unnoticed in caregivers' lives.

"AS THE JOURNEY ENDS:
PREPARING FOR WHEN
CAREGIVING IS OVER."

How to use this book:

This book will assist full-time caregivers who are considering caregiving or are already in the midst of caring for someone. With this book you will:

- Explore the various emotions full-time caregivers experience
- Learn ways to overcome the effects of those emotions
- Relate with other caregivers through the many stories shared
- Review the Frequently Asked Questions (FAQ's) which gives a concise summary of each emotion discussed.

Repeated throughout the book are reminders that being a caregiver is challenging and rewarding, that self-care is essential to both those we care for as well as the caregiver, and being proactive in seeking support from others including family, friends and professionals is key to effective caregiving.

We begin by noting caregiving has an often-quiet, unintentional beginning in **"A Quiet Beginning:** *The Undiscovered Course of Caregiving"*. In this chapter we point out the benefits of caregiving, the rewards of caregiving and the joys during the journey.

We then address the silence that surrounds caregiving, shedding light on the silent struggles that caregivers endure every day in **"The Silent Struggle:** *Unveiling the Emotional Turmoil of Caregivers"*. We dive deep into some of the emotions that surround caregiving.

Breaking the stigma around prioritizing the importance of mental health in caregivers is the focus of **"Breaking the Stigma:** *The Importance of Strengthening Your Mental Health"*. We provide practical strategies to help caregivers prioritize their mental and emotional well-being, without feeling guilty or ashamed. Also, everyday challenges can be a source of constant stress for caregivers. We explore different approaches to self-care that can help caregivers manage their emotions, reduce stress, and stay positive through difficult times.

We address the importance of building a support network, so caregivers don't have to face these challenges alone. In **"Finding Strength in Community:** *Building a Support Network for Caregivers"*, we explore the benefits of support groups, connecting with others who share similar experiences, and finding a supportive community.

Finally, **"As The Journey Ends:** *Preparing for When Caregiving is Over"*. Things to consider as your caregiving journey comes to an end.

If you are a full-time caregiver, this book is for you. We hope that you will find comfort, reassurance, and practical solutions to help you navigate the emotional challenges of caregiving.

How Many Caregivers in the U.S.?

Approximately 43.5 million caregivers have provided unpaid care to an adult or child in the last 12 months. *[National Alliance for Caregiving and AARP. (2015). Caregiving in the U.S.]*

About 34.2 million Americans have provided unpaid care to an adult age 50 or older in the last 12 months. *[National Alliance for Caregiving and AARP. (2015). Caregiving in the U.S.]*

The majority of caregivers (82%) care for one other adult, while 15% care for 2 adults, and 3% for 3 or more adults. *[National Alliance for Caregiving and AARP. (2015). Caregiving in the U.S.]*

Approximately 39.8 million caregivers provide care to adults (aged 18+) with a disability or illness or 16.6% of Americans. *[Coughlin, J. (2010). Estimating the Impact of Caregiving and Employment on Well-Being: Outcomes & Insights in Health Management.]*

About 15.7 million adult family caregivers care for someone who has Alzheimer's disease or other dementia. *[Alzheimer's Association. (2015). 2015 Alzheimer's Disease Facts and Figures.]*

Chapter 1: A Quiet Beginning:
The Undiscovered Course of Caregiving

As a caregiver for an elderly relative, it can feel like the weight of the world is on your shoulders. You want to provide the best possible care, but you may not know what that entails. **Before you jump into full-time caregiving, there are several things you should be aware of.**

Evaluate your own health and well-being

Caregiving can be physically and emotionally taxing. It's important to make sure you are in good health before taking on this responsibility. This includes getting enough sleep, eating well, and exercising regularly. Don't be afraid to ask for help if you need it.

Understand your loved one's medical needs

It's crucial to have a thorough understanding of your loved one's medical needs before entering into full-time caregiving. This includes any medications they may be taking, any medical conditions they may have, and any special dietary requirements.

1

Make sure you have a clear plan in place for managing their medical care.

Create a schedule and routine

Creating a schedule and routine can help both you and your loved one adjust to the new caregiving arrangement. This can include setting specific times for meals, medications, and activities. It's important to be flexible and adaptable, but having a basic routine in place can help provide structure and stability.

"YOU DON'T HAVE TO
GO THROUGH
THIS DARK TUNNEL ALONE."

Educate yourself on caregiving best practices

There is a wealth of information available on best practices for caregiving. This may include techniques for managing common issues such as dementia or incontinence, tips for preventing falls, or advice on how to provide emotional support. Seek out resources such as support groups or online forums to connect with other caregivers and learn from their experiences.

Take care of yourself

Finally, it's important to remember to take care of yourself as well. This may mean taking breaks when you need them, making time for your own hobbies and interests, or seeking out professional counseling if necessary. Remember, you can't take care of someone else if you're not taking care of yourself.

By taking the time to understand your loved one's needs, creating a routine, educating yourself, and prioritizing self-care, you can provide the best possible care and ensure a positive experience for both you and your loved one.

How Did I Get Here?

How did I become a caregiver? Was it something I chose, or was it simply a responsibility thrust upon me? However, it was an undiscovered area of my life. I've never been down this road before.

Growing up, my mother was always the rock of our family. She was the one who took care of me when I was sick, cooked our meals, and made sure I had everything I needed. She was the one who attended every school play, teacher's conference, and sports event that I participated in.

Dad was there, but he was always too tired from working overtime and never took time off for vacations or even when he was sick. It was his dedication to taking care of the family that sent him to an early grave at age 56.

But as mom got older, things changed. Her health began to decline, and suddenly, it was my turn to take care of her, as I was the only child.

At first, it was just trivial things. I would drive her to doctor's appointments, help her with her groceries, and make sure she was taking her medication on time. But as time went on, her needs grew, and so did my responsibilities.

Life has a way of rudely disrupting our journey without apologies.

It became very hard to form serious relationships, attend social events or even have time to myself. I was hampered with making sure mom was taken care of or burdened with guilt of even thinking about enjoying myself.

Now, I'm here almost every day, making sure she eats, helping her with her hygiene, and keeping her company.

It's not always easy, and there are days when I feel like I'm drowning in the weight of it all. But then I think about all the things my mother did for me when I was growing up, and I know that I can't let her down now.

Being a caregiver is a hard and often thankless job, but it's also one of the most gratifying things I've ever done. It's taught me patience, compassion, and the importance of putting others before myself. And when my mother looks up at me with those tired, grateful eyes, I know that every sacrifice I've made has been worth it.

So how did I get here? I suppose it was a combination of fate, circumstance, and love. But whatever the reason, as difficult as it is, I wouldn't trade this experience for anything in the world.

There are many ways that people become caregivers. Some become caregivers out of necessity, because a loved one becomes ill, injured, or disabled and needs their help. Others may become caregivers because they feel a sense of duty or responsibility to care for an aging or ill family member.

Some ways people become caregivers are:

Family caregiving: Often, family members become caregivers for a loved one who needs assistance due to a chronic illness, disability, or aging. This can include providing physical care, emotional support, and assistance with activities of daily living.

Professional caregiving: Professional caregivers are individuals who are trained to provide care to others, often in a healthcare setting. This can include nurses, home health aides, personal care assistants, and other healthcare professionals.

Volunteer caregiving: Some people become caregivers as volunteers, helping others in their community who need help.

This can include visiting elderly or disabled individuals, providing transportation, or helping with errands and household tasks.

Caregiving for children: Parents and other family members may become caregivers for children who have special needs, such as developmental disabilities, chronic illnesses, or behavioral issues.

"SMALL ACTS OF KINDNESS
CAN MAKE ALL THE DIFFERENCE
IN A CAREGIVER'S DAY."

No matter how someone becomes a caregiver, it is a role that requires patience, compassion, and dedication.

Often, a caregiver will experience being unappreciated by the one they are caring for. Although they have become the primary caregiver, fulfilling the person's every need, they can often be met with hostility and sometimes physical harm. It's easy to say it is not to be taken personally, but the truth is, it still hurts.

Let's look at the caregiver's journey with the rewards and benefits of caregiving. There are significant benefits for the caregiver as well as those who are being cared for.

Being a caregiver is more than just employment or a menial task to perform. One must recognize that it is a calling with a higher purpose. It requires tremendous strength, empathy, compassion, and patience. It's not an easy task, but it's a gift that can bring joy and fulfillment to you and the person you care for.

Caregiving is a Calling

Here is a story about a woman named Carol who had dedicated her life to caring for others. She had a big heart and a nurturing spirit that made her perfect for the job. For many years, she worked as a nurse in a hospital, but eventually she became bored with the routine day in and day out. "I need to do something that I enjoy and that I can make my own decisions." She decided to start her own home care business.

At first, it was hard for Carol to get her business off the ground. But slowly, she built up a roster of clients who relied on her to help them with their daily needs. She would spend her days cooking meals, doing laundry, and helping her clients with their personal care. She also made sure to spend time with them, listening to their stories and providing companionship.

Despite the challenges, Carol found great joy in her work. She often told her friends and family, "I love being able to make a difference in the lives of my clients, particularly those who were elderly and living alone." She knew that her presence in their lives meant the world to them, and that brought her a sense of purpose and fulfillment that she had never experienced before. She convinced those who doubted her at first that she had finally come into her own place in life.

One of her clients, a sweet elderly woman named Helene, became particularly dear to her. Helene had no family nearby and had become increasingly isolated in her home. But with Carol's help, Helene was able to maintain her independence and continue living in her own home. They would spend hours chatting and laughing together, and Carol often brought her favorite treats to share.

One day, Helene's health took a turn for the worse. Carol was devastated, but she was determined to be there for her until the very end. She spent long hours at Helene's bedside, holding her hand and comforting her. When Helene passed away, Carol was heartbroken, but she knew that she had made a difference in her life.

In the end, Carol realized that caregiving was a way for her to live out her values of compassion and service, and to make a difference in the world. She continued to care for others for many years, grateful for the opportunity to bring joy and comfort to those who needed it most. Carol remarked, "I finally found what I was looking for.

Caregiving is not just a job, but a calling."Caregiving may not be the most glamorous job, but it is undoubtedly one of the most purposeful. The act of providing care can give you a sense of meaning and purpose that few other jobs can offer. Every task, no matter how small, has the potential to create a positive impact in the life of the person you care for.

"CAREGIVER IS A ROLE THAT REQUIRES PATIENCE, COMPASSION, AND DEDICATION."

There is also the joy of making a difference. Few professions can give one the opportunity to connect with others and make a difference in their lives. When you provide exceptional care, you can create a positive change in the world. Whether you're caring for a family member, friend, or stranger, the impact of your work can be immeasurable. The feeling of satisfaction that comes from making a meaningful difference in someone's life is unparalleled.

Caring... In Spite Of

Kenisha, an African American caregiver had been in the caregiving profession for over a decade. She had encountered all types of clients, from the sweetest old ladies to the grumpiest old men. But one day, she was introduced to a new client, a 101-year-old white woman named Elizabeth, by her son Christopher.

As soon as Kenisha entered the room, Elizabeth started yelling and using racial slurs, including the n-word, telling her to leave and that she didn't want a "black person" in her house. Kenisha was taken aback and hurt by the woman's words, but she knew that this was not about her personally, but rather a reflection of the prejudices that Elizabeth had grown up with.

"DON'T BE AFRAID TO ASK FOR HELP IF YOU NEED IT."

Despite the initial hostility, Kenisha resolved to be patient and compassionate with Elizabeth. She started by trying to find common ground with her, asking about her background and interests. As she listened to Elizabeth's stories about growing up in the deep south, being raised by parents who were racially intolerant, she began to realize that there was more to her than just her racist beliefs. Elizabeth spoke of her mother very fondly and told how she was taught to cook and sew, as well as how to be a "lady" in social settings.

Over time, Elizabeth's behavior towards Kenisha improved, and they even developed a close bond. Kenisha would bring her small gifts and treats, and they would spend hours chatting and laughing together. Christopher was amazed by the transformation and how much happier his mother was with Kenisha around.

One day, Christopher pulled Kenisha aside and asked her how she was able to deal with his mother's initial behavior. Kenisha replied, "To do this job, you need a little Jesus and a lot of patience." She explained that she had learned to not take things personally and to approach each client with empathy and understanding.

"CHALLENGES CAN ALSO BE VALUABLE."

In the end, Kenisha's patience and compassion had paid off, and she had not only earned Elizabeth's trust and respect but also helped her to overcome some of her prejudices. It was a reminder that sometimes, the hardest people to love are the ones who need it the most.

The Challenges of Caregiving

Caregiving is one of the most unsettling jobs you can do. There are long hours, unpredictable behaviors, and the stress of knowing that your loved one's wellbeing is in your hands. It can be especially exhausting when you're caring for someone with dementia or other cognitive impairments, as their needs can change rapidly, and it can be hard to communicate with them.

But challenges can also be valuable. They force us to grow and develop new skills, both as caregivers and as individuals. And when we rise to the challenges of caregiving, we can find great satisfaction and even joy in our work.

The Challenges of Autism

Living on a beautiful 2.5-acre farm near Moorestown, New Jersey, Joyce enjoys watching the birds and the comings and goings of wildlife, but daily life can be hard. Jerome, her son, is a bright boy with autism, and has difficulty with social and communication skills. He is active and playful, but can be unpredictable, which creates many challenges for Joyce, as well as his two brothers, Aaron and Anthony the twins, and their younger sister Charlotte.

"THERE IS ALSO THE JOY OF MAKING A DIFFERENCE."

Joyce had always known that raising Jerome would be a challenge. Jerome was diagnosed with autism at an early age. This developmental disorder affects his ability to interact with others, communicate effectively, and express his feelings. For many years, Jerome did not receive the support and understanding that he needed because his condition was not fully understood. This made life very difficult for him and his family.

Jerome was now 15 years old, but he still had the energy of a young child. He was constantly on the move, running around the house and yard, and Joyce struggled to keep up with him. She was exhausted from trying to keep him safe and entertained, and she often felt like she was failing.

The impact of autism on the entire family is significant. Aaron and Anthony help with the farm chores and strive to be supportive towards Jerome, but it can be tough for them to understand his needs. Charlotte sometimes feels neglected as Jerome gets most of their mom's attention. It creates a stressful dynamic when one member of the family requires so much attention and support. However, the family has learned to adapt, and everyone in the family has grown from handling the challenges they've faced together.

"It's hard," she told her friend Sarah one day as they sat in the kitchen drinking coffee. "I love him more than anything, but sometimes I feel like I can't do this anymore. He's so active, and I'm just so tired."

Sarah nodded sympathetically. "I can't even imagine," she said. "But you're doing an amazing job. You're an incredible mom."

Joyce smiled weakly, but she didn't feel like an incredible mom. She felt like she was barely keeping her head above water. And it wasn't just Jerome who was a challenge. Her other three children were also a handful.

The twins, Aaron and Anthony, were 17 years old and constantly bickering with each other. They were both involved in sports and had busy schedules, which made it difficult for Joyce to keep track of everything. And then there was Charlotte, who was 13 and going through a moody teenage phase.

"It's like a never-ending juggling act," Joyce said to her husband Allen over dinner one night. "I feel like I'm constantly trying to keep everyone happy and I'm failing at it."

Allen reached across the table and took her hand. "You're not failing," he said. "You're doing the best you can. And we'll figure this out together."

But even with Allen's support, Joyce still felt over-whelmed. She struggled to find time for herself, and she often felt guilty for not being able to give each of her children the attention they deserved.

"It's like I'm always putting out fires," she said to her sister-in-law one day. "I can't even think about the future because I'm so focused on getting through each day."

"IT'S WORTH IT,
WHEN I SEE JEROME SMILE."

Her sister-in-law nodded sympathetically. "It's tough," she said. "But you're doing an amazing job. You're a warrior."

Joyce appreciated the kind words, but she didn't feel like a warrior. She felt like a woman who was barely keeping it together. But then, one day, something shifted.

Jerome had always struggled with communication, but he had recently started using a communication device that allowed him to express himself more fully. He started to share his thoughts and feelings, and Joyce was amazed by what he had to say.

"He's so much smarter than we thought," she said to her husband one night. "He's been trapped in his own world for so long, but now he's starting to break free."

And as Jerome started to express himself more fully, Joyce started to feel like she was making progress. She started to see the challenges as opportunities, and she started to appreciate the little moments of joy that came with caring for a child with autism.

"It's not easy," she said to her friend Sarah one day. "But it's worth it when I see Jerome smile. Despite the challenges, the love and strength of family are what keep Jerome and his family going. The bond they create during their challenges develops their strength and motivates them to dedicate themselves to Jerome's needs."

Finding Support and Resources

Finding support and resources is essential for parents of a child with autism. Many organizations, such as the Autism Society of America offer a wide variety of services and resources for families affected by autism. Joyce has connected with other autism moms through social media, which occasionally helps her recharge from all the challenges of caregiving.

The Importance of Understanding and Acceptance

Understanding and acceptance are essential in helping Jerome and his family cope. It has been difficult to prevent people from treating him strangely, or bullying him due to their ignorance. Misunderstanding leads to fear of his unusual behaviors. The key to addressing this issue is through encouragement, awareness, and acceptance.

Coping Strategies for Parents of Children with Autism

To cope with the stress of caring for a child with autism, it's important to have a support system, avoid comparing your child to others, and create a predictable and stable routine. An essential part of any coping strategy is self-care for parents to avoid burnout.

The Role of Education and Therapy

Education and therapy play a significant role in helping children with autism. Jerome is attending a specialized educational program that has allowed him to develop more new skills. Therapy has also help him understand when someone will stroke him, for example, as it used to make him uncomfortable. However, he has improved over time.

Dementia's Devastating Demands
The Dark Truth About Caregiving

Caregiving for a loved one can be an incredibly challenging and difficult experience, both physically and emotionally. However, what happens when the person you are caring for begins to show signs of dementia? Gertrude, a 78-year-old with chronic conditions, had been under the care of Vanessa, a full-time caregiver, for three years. But when the signs of dementia started to appear, their caregiving journey took a devastating turn. This is Gertrude's story.

Gertrude was a fiercely independent woman, but her chronic conditions made it difficult for her to carry out daily tasks. Vanessa had been recommended to Gertrude by a friend, and she started working as her full-time caregiver, coming in daily for five hours. Vanessa was a caring and attentive caregiver, providing Gertrude with all the assistance she needed. In the beginning, the relationship between Gertrude and Vanessa was one of mutual respect and camaraderie.

Things began to change when Gertrude started showing signs of dementia. At first, it was small things like forgetfulness or confusion, which Vanessa didn't think much of. As time went by, Gertrude's condition started to deteriorate. She would require more attention and assistance, and Vanessa wasn't prepared for the mental changes that accompanied dementia.

As Gertrude's condition worsened, Vanessa became increasingly frustrated, impatient, and irritable. She found it difficult to deal with Gertrude's behavior, which was out of character and, at times, seemed completely irrational. Gertrude would accuse Vanessa of mistreatment and stealing, even though it was clear that Vanessa was doing everything within her power to take care of her.

Vanessa soon realized that Gertrude's behavior was the result of dementia-induced paranoia, and this manifested in different phases of dementia. Gertrude could be combative in one instance and then very docile and cooperative in another. These mood swings required Vanessa to be on alert all the time, which was mentally exhausting.

Gertrude's dementia demands captivated Vanessa's life. She stopped doing normal activities, stopped going out to see friends and became fully immersed in caregiving. Gertrude demanded all of Vanessa's time leaving no room for any breaks or time of rest. The situation worsened when Gertrude became physically abusive and struck Vanessa several times. This lead Vanessa to feel helpless, and she didn't know how to provide care to an unresponsive and violent patient. It changed her life and was a turning point in their relationship.

Gertrude passed away a few months later. The experience left Vanessa shattered both emotionally and mentally. She was left with a feeling of resentment toward dementia for taking the person she had known. Gertrude had been with her on this journey for three years. During that time, both women relied on one another for emotional support. In the end, Gertrude's dementia consumed them both, leaving behind an ugly ending to their relationship.

The story of Gertrude and Vanessa highlights the difficulties and complexities of caregiving, especially when dementia is involved. It's never an easy task to provide care for someone who has lost an important part of themselves. But with patience, understanding, and compassion, caregivers can make the journey a little bit easier.

Frequently Asked Questions: (FAQs)

What is dementia?

Dementia is a term used to describe a range of symptoms associated with a decline in memory or other thinking skills. These symptoms are severe enough to reduce daily functioning.

What are some common signs of dementia?

Some common signs of dementia include forgetfulness, difficulty remembering names, places, or recent events, and difficulty communicating.

What are some strategies for coping with difficult behavior in patients with dementia?

There are several strategies caregivers can use to manage difficult behavior in patients with dementia. These strategies include redirecting the patient's attention, re framing the situation in a positive, light validating the patient's feelings, and maintaining a calm and positive attitude throughout.

How can I manage my own stress levels while caring for a loved one with dementia?

Caring for a loved one with dementia can be a demanding and stressful experience. Caregivers should try to take regular breaks, practice self-care, and seek support from friends, family, or a counselor if needed.

Finding Joy in Caregiving

One way to find joy in caregiving is to focus on the positive moments. Even if your loved one is having a bad day, there are always small blessings to be found. Maybe you shared a laugh over a silly joke, or they enjoyed a good meal that you prepared. Take the time to appreciate these moments and cherish them.

Embracing the Journey

As a caregiver, one of the most important things you can do is to embrace the journey that lies ahead of you. Caring for a loved one, whether it's an aging parent or a child with special needs, can be an incredibly demanding experience. However, it's also an experience that can be incredibly rewarding, both for the caregiver and the person being cared for. We will explore the importance of embracing the journey of caregiving, recognizing that it's a long-term commitment filled with ups and downs along the way. We'll also examine the rewards of caregiving and discuss how you can find meaning and fulfillment in this demanding but ultimately fulfilling role.

"UNDERSTANDING AND ACCEPTANCE ARE ESSENTIAL."

The Ups and Downs of Caregiving

Caregiving can be a roller coaster ride, with highs and lows that can be difficult to navigate. There will be times when you feel overwhelmed, exhausted, and frustrated – times when you question whether you're up to the task of providing care. But there will also be moments of joy, connection, and profound meaning that make the experience deeply gratifying. The key is to recognize that both the ups and downs are a normal part of the caregiving journey, and that embracing them both is essential to finding purpose and fulfillment in your role.

The Rewards of Caregiving

Despite the many challenges of caregiving, there are also countless rewards that come with the territory. For many caregivers, the most powerful reward is the deep sense of connection and purpose that comes from caring for a loved one. When you're providing care for someone you love, you're helping them navigate a difficult time in their lives, and that can be an incredibly meaningful experience. Additionally, caregiving can also bring tangible rewards, such as financial compensation or access to support services that can help ease the burden of care.

Unexpected Humor

Being a family caregiver comes with its share of difficulties, but there are also moments of unexpected humor that can help brighten even the darkest days. I remember a time when my elderly mother, who was suffering from dementia, began to walk around the living room with her slippers on the wrong feet. At first, I was worried that something was seriously wrong, but then I couldn't help but chuckle at her quirkiness. It was a small moment of levity that reminded me that there was still joy and humor to be found in our shared journey.

"OFTEN, FAMILY MEMBERS BECOME CAREGIVERS FOR A LOVED ONE WHO NEEDS ASSISTANCE"

Sunday Shoes

The story of Aunt Joanne and her nephew Brian is one that embodies humor and the warmth of family love.

It is a funny tale depicting the caregiving journey of a demented elderly aunt and her dedicated nephew. Aunt Joanne a 96-year-old woman with dementia, resides with her 52-year-old nephew. She frequently experiences senior moments, often mixing up her things, her routine, and occasionally even her shoes. Fortunately, her nephew or another family member is always present to lend a helping hand.

"EMBRACE THE JOURNEY THAT LIES AHEAD OF YOU."

One morning, Brian was helping Jo with her morning routine, preparing for the day, as he had done many times before. Jo asked her nephew to get her coffee, which was a regular request every morning. The nephew started brewing the coffee Jo went to the living room to read the daily papers.

When the coffee was finally ready, the nephew went to the living room to serve Jo. However, he saw her sitting on the couch with a worried expression on her face. She was wearing two different types of shoes-one black one and one brown.

After greeting her and placing the coffee mug on the table, he pointed out, "Aunt Jo, I believe you are wearing two different shoes today." Aunt Jo looked down at her feet, puzzled for a moment, and then exclaimed, "Oh dear! I must have put on my shoes in the dark this morning!"

"But why did you put on your church shoes this morning?",
he gently inquired.

Just realizing it wasn't Sunday, she cleverly replied, "Well,
I just wanted to make sure they still fit."

Brian couldn't help but chuckle at her response, and the
two shared a good laugh together. From then on, Brian
made sure to double-check Aunt Joanne's shoes before
they left the house each day just in case she decided to
get dressed "in the dark" again.

Joanne continues to live with her nephew, and they
share many funny moments together, even in difficult
circumstances. The story is a reminder of the importance
of family, the warmth of love, and learning to appreciate
the funny moments in our lives.

The Beauty of Simple Pleasures

As caregivers, we need to learn to appreciate the beauty of
simple pleasures. Taking a walk outside or sitting in the sun
may seem like small acts, but they can bring a sense of peace
and serenity amidst the chaos of caregiving. Sitting on a bench
listening to the birds chirping, watching the children playing,
and feeling the warmth of the sun on your face are invaluable
experiences that can drastically change your perspective. It's the
simple pleasures of life that can make a vast difference.

Creating Meaningful Shared Experiences

As a caregiver, is crucial to discover ways to establish significant share experiences with your loved one. Even basic
activities such watching a favorite movie or cooking a favorite
meal together can create lasting memories and bring a sense of
bonding and connection. Occasionally, in the most challenging
times of caregiving, a ray of light can merge. The following is
one such experience:

The Power of Cooking With Love

Leonard always dreamed of becoming a chef. Growing up, he would avidly watch cooking shows, including those hosted by Emeril Lagasse and Paula Dean. He was particularly fond of Emeril's enthusiastic "bam" when he adding spices to his dishes.

Leonard was fortunate enough to attend The Restaurant School at Walnut Hill College in Philadelphia where he studied Culinary Arts and Restaurant Management, with the hope of one day opening his own restaurant.

However, as life often does, it took a different turn. Leonard met a beautiful young woman, Victoria, and they had a whirlwind romance that led to marriage, all within the same year. While Leonard continued to cook for family and friends, his dream of owning a restaurant took a backseat. He needed to support his growing family so he traded his chef skills for a job at Tastykake Baking Company where he made delectable pastries like Krimpets and Juniors.

Despite these changes, Leonard and Victoria remained a fun-loving couple. They enjoyed spending time in downtown Philly not only dining at elegant restaurants but also grabbing lunch at the counter tops in Reading Terminal. Whenever they visited there, they would buy fresh groceries allowing Leonard to again feel like a chef at home when cooking for his family.

One day after having a routine physical, Victoria received devastating news that every couple hoped they would never receive: stage four breast cancer. The dreaded disease progressed rapidly and soon, even with all available treatments, she was placed under hospice care.

The aides and hospice staff were more than comforting and supportive throughout the entire ordeal. Leonard too, found himself cooking meals not only for Victoria, but shared with those who were at home at the time. It became a beloved ritual for Leonard to prepare a chef's specialty every single night for his wife, as well as the hospice staff and aids.

And then it dawned on everyone. Victoria, although visibly declining, managed to maintain her appetite and enjoy the exquisite meals prepared by her loving and attentive husband. Even Leonard remarked, "I thought for sure she wouldn't be able to eat solid foods by now, but look at her; she's enjoying every bite." Of course, he had to carefully cut some of the salmon and other portions into smaller pieces for Vicky, but the flavor and ambiance remained as grand as ever.

Eventually, Vicky finally succumbed to the relentless disease, breaking the hearts of everyone who cared for her. But then something miraculous happened. Leonard, through his devoted care and meticulous meal preparations, rediscovered his dream of becoming a chef.

With a portion of the insurance they had purchased when they first got married, he was able to acquire and run his own gourmet restaurant. Combining the skills he had learned at both the restaurant school and Tastykake, his restaurant, appropriately named Vicky's Grill and Bakery, became the go-to place for dining and socializing downtown. Even amidst the tragedy of losing someone so dear, caregiving for loved ones can prove to be a wonderful, and rewarding life experience.

Discovering Moments of Grace

Moments of grace can be found in unexpected places, and as a caregiver, it's important to stay open to them. Whether it's a friendly face, a kind word, or a shared smile, these small acts of kindness can make all the difference in a caregiver's day.

I recently needed to make an appointment for a minor medical procedure so I called the scheduler for the MRI department. However, I was immediately put on hold. I waited for what seemed like an inhumanly long time, which made me very irate. Finally, a real person's voice came on the line and apologized for the long wait.

"THE JOB OF A CAREGIVER IS A NOBLE ONE."

I suddenly found myself faced with a decision: should I make her pay for the numerous annoying on hold messages, or should I turn the situation around to my advantage? Without hesitation, I swiftly responded to her barrage of verification questions. However, I paused when she inquired about any metal in my body, such as fragments from gunshots. "Well, I haven't been to Philly recently, considering the bulletproof vest I ordered was on back ordered." I quipped, I could hear a faint chuckle as she continued her "interrogation". "Sir, what's your height and weight?" It was at that moment I decided to inject some creativity into the conversation, just for the sake of amusement. "Well, I'm 5'9", and weigh 215 pounds, but I just can't seem to get rid of this gut!" I proceeded to explain, "I've tried everything from fasting to concoctions that promise weight loss, but nothing seems to be working. Do you have any suggestions?

We continued joking for a few minutes, secured an appointment and I was assured that the gut situation would not be part of my medical history. By the end of the call, we both appreciated the humor that arose from a potentially volatile situation. I was able to return my caregiving duties with a smile, for a change.of my medical history.

As caregivers, we must never underestimate the power of moments of grace in providing a sense of joy and meaning in our daily experiences. By staying open to the moments of humor, connection, and kindness that come our way, we can navigate the challenges of caregiving with a greater sense of hope and optimism.

"CAREGIVERS MAY FEEL FRUSTRATION."

Finding Meaning and Fulfillment in Caregiving

To find meaning and fulfillment in caregiving, it's important to approach the role with mindfulness and intention. This entails taking the time to reflect on your motivations for caregiving, and carefully considering the values that guide your approach to care.

By treating caregiving as a spiritual practice, and being mindful of your own needs and limitations, you can discover find deeper meaning and fulfillment in the role. Furthermore, it is crucial to seek support and connect with other caregivers, who can offer a valuable source of community and encouragement.

Remember, caregiving is a long-term commitment that comes with both challenges and rewards. By embracing the journey of caregiving and facing both the ups and downs with mindfulness and intention, you can find deep meaning and fulfillment in this important role. Whether you're caring for a loved one with a chronic illness, or providing support for an aging parent, remember that the journey itself can be rewarding, even during difficult times.

Chapter 2: The Silent Struggle:
Unveiling the Emotional Turmoil of Caregivers

As a caregiver, you are a hero for the person you care for, but often an unsung silent hero for society. The job of a caregiver is noble, but it can also be strenuous and draining. Caregiving can take a toll on one's mental, physical, and emotional health. Being a caregiver can feel like an emotional roller coaster, with many ups and downs. Caregivers are often responsible for meeting the physical, emotional, and social needs of their loved ones, which can be a stressful task. In this article, we will explore the hidden emotions of full-time caregivers, the pain points they face, and provide practical solutions to help them cope.

Here are some of the emotions that caregivers commonly experience:

Anxiety and stress: Caregiving can be a source of anxiety and stress, especially when the caregiver is responsible for managing complex medical or financial issues. Caregivers may worry about their loved one's health and well-being, and they may also worry about their own ability to cope with the demands of caregiving.

Frustration and anger: Caregiving can be frustrating and stressful, particularly when the person being cared for is uncooperative or difficult to manage. At times, caregivers may feel angry or resentful, especially if they feel their efforts are not appreciated.

"OFTEN A CAREGIVER WILL EXPERIENCE BEING UNAPPRECIATED."

Guilt and self-doubt: Many caregivers experience feelings of guilt and self-doubt, especially if they believe they are not adequately caring for their loved one. They may question their own abilities and feel guilty when they need to take a break or ask for help.

Joy and fulfillment: Despite the challenges, many caregivers find joy and fulfillment in their role. They may feel proud and accomplished in caring for their loved one, and they may also find meaning and purpose in their caregiving role.

Love and affection: Caregivers often have a deep love and affection for the person they care for. This love can be a source of joy and fulfillment, and can provide them with the strength and motivation to continue caring for their loved one even in seemingly impossible circumstances.

"CAREGIVERS MAY FEEL HELPLESS."

Sadness and grief: Caregivers may experience feelings of sadness and grief as they watch their loved one's health decline. They may also feel a sense of loss as they give up their own personal goals and dreams to care for their loved one.

Overall, being a caregiver can be a complex and emotionally draining experience, with characterized by numerous highs and lows. It is important for caregivers to prioritize self-care and seek support when needed to help manage and effectively cope with the emotional demands of caregiving.

Uncovering the Hidden Emotions of Full-Time Caregivers:

When caring for a loved one, full-time caregivers are likely to experience a range of emotions. They may have to deal with feelings of abandonment, anger, anxiety, depression, exhaustion, fear, frustration, grief, guilt, helplessness, hopelessness, loneliness, regret, stress, and worry to name a few. Caregivers may feel guilty because they are unable to provide the level of care they want to. Grief may arise because of the loss of a loved one's abilities or the decline in their health. Fear may surface because of worrying about the future and what it may hold. Frustration may occur from the lack of control when dealing with someone else's health. Furthermore, caregivers may feel anger towards the person they are caring for and towards themselves.

Perhaps the following story will help reveal some of these emotions and the process that causes many caregivers to experience feelings of hopelessness.

Sonia's Emotional Journey

Sonia, a devoted daughter decided to rearrange her life to take care of her elderly mother who suffered from dementia. Sonia had always been close to her mother and felt it was her duty to provide her with the best care possible. However, the journey was not an easy one.

"CAREGIVING REQUIRES A GREAT DEAL OF EMPATHY."

At first, Sonia felt a deep sense of purpose and fulfillment in caring for her mother. She enjoyed spending time with her and taking care of her needs. However, as her mother's condition worsened, Sonia began to feel overwhelmed and stressed. She was constantly worried about her mother's safety and well-being and struggled to balance her caregiving responsibilities with her own personal life.

As the months went by, Sonia's emotions became a roller coaster ride. Some days, she felt grateful for the opportunity to care for her mother and was able to find joy in the little moments they shared together. However, on other days, she felt angry, frustrated, and exhausted, resenting the huge burden that had been placed on her shoulders.

Sonia's emotional journey was also impacted by the changes in her mother's condition. There were moments of clarity when her mother recognized her, and they were able to connect on a deep level. But there were also times when her mother became agitated and confused, lashing out at Sonia and making her feel helpless and powerless.

Despite the challenges, Sonia persevered. She sought support from other caregivers and joined a local support group where she could share her experiences and connect with others who understood what she was going through. She also made sure to take time for herself, finding small moments of joy in hobbies and activities that brought her happiness.

In the end, Sonia's journey as a caregiver was a bittersweet one. It was filled with both moments of love and joy, as well as moments of sadness and frustration. But through it all, she learned the true meaning of compassion and selflessness, and was able to find a deep sense of purpose in caring for her mother in her time of need.

"CAREGIVERS SHOULD PRACTICE SELF-COMPASSION."

It's important to understand that these emotions are normal and reasonable. Caregivers should practice self-compassion and remind themselves that they are doing the best they can with the resources they have. Some ways to cope with emotions include keeping a journal, seeking professional help, and connecting with others in similar situations.

Let's examine some of these emotions and the stories that convey the experiences of caregivers. We will explore the clinical definitions, the affects these emotions may have, and offer tips on how to cope when these emotions arise. Additionally, we will include We will also provide FAQs at the end of each emotion topic for concise answers regarding the emotional needs of their loved ones.

*In the upcoming section, we'll delve into
15 emotions frequently encountered
by full-time caregivers.*

- Abandonment
- Anger
- Anxiety
- Depression
- Exhaustion
- Fear
- Frustration
- Grief
- Guilt
- Helplessness
- Hopelessness
- Loneliness
- Regret
- Stress
- Worry

ABANDONMENT

The feeling of being abandoned or experiencing abandonment according to full-time caregivers can be described as a sense of isolation or being left alone to manage the responsibilities of caregiving without sufficient support or resources. Caregivers may feel overwhelmed, unsupported, and emotionally drained, as they often have to sacrifice their own needs and desires to provide care for their loved ones. These feelings can be intensified when caregivers feel that their efforts are not recognized or appreciated by others and when they lack access to adequate resources such as respite care, counseling, or financial support. Overall, the feeling of abandonment can be a significant source of stress and emotional burden for full-time caregivers, and it is important for them to seek out support to prevent burnout.

These feelings may arise due to a variety of factors, including the caregiver feeling like they are not receiving enough support or recognition for their efforts, or feeling like they are carrying the burden of caregiving alone.

Here are some ways that feelings of abandonment can present themselves in caregiving, as well as some strategies for managing these feelings:

Emotional distance: Caregivers may feel emotionally distant from their loved one, particularly if their loved one is unable to express gratitude or appreciation for the care they are receiving.

Social isolation: Caregivers may feel socially isolated if they are unable to participate in social activities or if they feel like they cannot leave their loved one alone.

Resentment: Caregivers may feel resentful toward family members or friends who are not helping with caregiving responsibilities, leading to feelings of abandonment.

Burnout: Caregivers may experience burnout if they feel like they are carrying the burden of caregiving alone, leading to feelings of exhaustion and emotional depletion.

"CAREGIVERS MAY FEEL RESENTFUL."

Reasons A Caregiver May Be Abandoned

Often one who becomes the sole caregiver may be abandoned by the rest of the family. **Some possible reasons include:**

Lack of awareness: Some family members may not fully understand the extent of care that is required for the person in need, or they may not understand the burden that the sole caregiver is facing.

Distance: Family members who live far away from the person in need may not be able to provide physical support and may not fully appreciate the challenges of caregiving from a distance.

Personal issues: Family members may have their own personal issues or commitments that prevent them from providing the necessary support, or they may have strained relationships with the caregiver or the person in need.

Lack of resources: Some family members may not have the financial or other resources to provide support, or they may not have access to the necessary resources to help the caregiver.

Burnout: Caregiving can be emotionally and physically exhausting, and some family members may feel overwhelmed and unable to provide the necessary support.

It's important to note that every family is unique, and there may be other factors at play that contribute to why some family members may abandon the sole caregiver. It's important for families to communicate openly and honestly about their needs and limitations, and to work together to provide the best possible care for their loved ones.

Even when the caregiver is not literally abandoned, often the feelings of abandonment surface. It can happen when the caregiver feels burned out or overwhelmed by the demands of caregiving, or when they feel that they are not appreciated or valued. It can also happen when the caregiver is dealing with their own personal problems or when they feel that their efforts are not making a difference.

Whatever the cause, abandonment is a serious issue for both the caregiver and the person they are caring for. It can lead to feelings of guilt, anxiety, and depression, and it can also impact the quality of care that the caregiver is able to provide.

Signs of Abandonment

There are several signs that a full-time caregiver may be experiencing abandonment.

These include:

- Feeling overwhelmed or unable to cope

- Feeling like nobody appreciates their efforts

- Feeling guilty or ashamed about their role as a caregiver

- Becoming impatient or irritable with the person they are caring for

- Feeling resentful of the person they are caring for

- Neglecting their own self-care, such as not eating properly or not getting enough sleep.

If you are a full-time caregiver and you are experiencing any of these signs, it is important to seek help.

Abandoned, Yet Still Committed

Gregory had always been close to his grandfather Arthur. They would spend hours talking about the old days, sharing stories and laughing together. But as Arthur began to age and his health declined, Gregory found himself taking on more and more responsibility for his care.

At first, it was just small things like picking up groceries or driving Arthur to doctor's appointments. But as Arthur's condition worsened, Gregory found himself becoming a full-time caregiver, with little support from his family.

Despite his best efforts, Gregory felt like he was constantly struggling to keep up with Arthur's needs. He would spend long hours each day helping him with everything from bathing and dressing to managing his medications and ensuring that he was getting proper nutrition.

To make matters worse, Gregory's wife was struggling with the caregiving responsibilities as well. She had initially been supportive of his decision to care for Arthur, but as the demands of caregiving grew more intense, she began to feel overwhelmed and resentful.

"OFTEN ONE WHO BECOMES THE SOLE CAREGIVER MAY BE ABANDONED BY THE REST OF THE FAMILY."

One day, Gregory's wife told him that she was leaving. She said that she couldn't handle the stress of caregiving and that she needed to focus on her own needs for a while. Gregory was devastated by the news, feeling like he had lost not only his wife but also his support system.

As time went on, Gregory became increasingly isolated and overwhelmed. His family members, who had initially promised to help, seemed to disappear when he needed them most. He was left alone to figure out how to care for his grandfather and manage his own emotions at the same time.

Despite the challenges, Gregory remained committed to caring for his grandfather. He knew that Arthur relied on him, and he didn't want to let him down. Over time, he found support in unexpected places, such as online caregiver support groups and local community organizations.

Although the journey was difficult, Gregory persevered. He learned to prioritize his own well-being and seek out the support he needed, and he continued to care for his grandfather with love and dedication until the end.

Caregiving can be an overwhelming and exhausting experience, especially when it feels like you're doing it alone.

If Gregory feels abandoned by his family, it may be helpful for him to reach out to them and express his feelings. It's possible that they simply don't realize how much he is struggling and may be willing to offer more support if they understand the gravity of the situation. Alternatively, there may be reasons why they are unable to help, such as work or other family commitments.

In addition to reaching out to his family, Gregory may also want to consider seeking support from outside sources. There are many organizations and resources available to caregivers that can provide guidance, advice, and emotional support. For example, the National Alliance for Caregiving offers a wealth of resources for caregivers, including support groups and educational materials.

Finally, it's important for Gregory to take care of his own well-being as well as that of his grandfather. Caregiver burnout is a real risk, and it's essential for Gregory to take breaks and find ways to recharge his batteries. This may mean taking advantage of respite care services, asking friends or neighbors for help, or simply taking some time for himself to relax and recharge.

It's important to note that abandoning a caregiver can have serious consequences for the person receiving care. If you are a caregiver who is struggling, it's important to reach out for help and support before making any decisions about stopping care.

Feelings of abandonment can have a significant impact on caregivers, who are often responsible for providing ongoing care and support to others. Caregivers who feel abandoned may experience a range of negative emotions, such as anxiety, depression, anger, and resentment. They may also feel overwhelmed and stressed, particularly if they feel they are solely responsible for providing care and support.

In some cases, caregivers may feel abandoned by the person they are caring for, particularly if that person is unable to express gratitude or appreciation for the care they are receiving. Caregivers may also feel abandoned by family members or friends who are not providing the support or assistance they need.

"CAREGIVERS OFTEN HAVE A DEEP LOVE AND AFFECTION FOR THE PERSON THEY ARE CARING FOR."

Feelings of abandonment can also lead to caregiver burnout, a state of physical, emotional, and mental exhaustion that can result from prolonged stress and the demands of caregiving. Caregiver burnout can cause a range of symptoms, such as fatigue, irritability, and decreased motivation.

If you are a full-time caregiver and you feel like you are experiencing abandonment, it is important to take action.

Some strategies that may be helpful include:

- Seeking help from a mental health professional

- Prioritizing your own self-care needs

- Reaching out to family and friends for support

- Talking to the person you are caring for about your feelings

- Considering taking a break from your caregiving role if necessary.

Remember, abandonment is a serious issue, but with the right strategies and support in place, it is possible to overcome abandonment and continue to provide high-quality care to the person you are caring for. If you are experiencing abandonment, remember to prioritize your own needs and seek help when necessary.

"CAREGIVERS
MAY FEEL ABANDONED
BY THE PERSON THEY ARE
CARING FOR."

Frequently Asked Questions: (FAQs)

What is abandonment in full-time caregivers?

Abandonment in full-time caregivers occurs when the caregiver feels like they are on their own and unsupported, leading to negative effects on both the caregiver and the person they are caring for.

What are the causes of abandonment in full-time caregivers?

Abandonment may be caused by burnout, feeling unappreciated or undervalued, dealing with personal problems, or feeling like their efforts are not making a difference.

Can abandonment in full-time caregivers be overcome?

Yes, abandonment can be overcome through seeking emotional support, prioritizing self-care, setting boundaries, developing a support system, and keeping a positive mind-set.

What are the signs of abandonment in full-time caregivers?

Signs of abandonment may include feeling overwhelmed or unable to cope, feeling like nobody appreciates their efforts, becoming irritable or impatient, and neglecting their own self-care.

Why is it important to address abandonment in full-time caregivers?

It is important to address abandonment in full-time caregivers because it can have a profound impact on both the caregiver and the person they are caring for, leading to negative consequences for everyone involved.

"Caregiving requires Patience."

ANGER

The feeling of being angry can vary for full-time caregivers depending on the situation and their individual experiences. However, some common definitions or descriptions of anger among full-time caregivers may include: Anger is a strong emotion characterized by feelings of frustration, irritation, and annoyance in response to a perceived injustice, unfairness, or lack of control; Anger is a natural response to the stress and demands of caregiving, such as when dealing with difficult behaviors or challenging medical conditions of the care recipient; Anger is a complex emotion that can be triggered by a range of factors, including feelings of guilt, grief, or overwhelm, as well as external factors such as lack of support or resources.

Overall, anger can be a normal and healthy response to certain situations, but it can also become problematic if it leads to aggressive or harmful behavior towards oneself or others. It is important for caregivers to recognize and manage their feelings of anger in a constructive and healthy way, with the help of support from others, self-care practices, and professional resources if needed.

As a full-time caregiver, it is not unusual to experience the perplexing and multifaceted emotion of anger. The task of caregiving is incredibly demanding and stressful, requiring intense physical and emotional energy. Consequently, feeling overwhelmed, frustrated, and experiencing moments of anger are common.

There are various reasons why anger can emerge, such as feeling unsupported or unappreciated by others, believing that it is impossible to alter the situation, or sensing that your own needs and desires are subordinated to the role of caregiving. Additionally, the person you are caring for could be the source of your anger, especially if they are in a situation where they cannot communicate or cooperate with you.

As a caregiver, it is important to acknowledge and recognize your anger instead of burying it. Failing to do so can lead to a heightened level of emotional strife and further tension. Nevertheless, managing your anger in a healthy way is crucial, as inappropriate expressions of anger can have an adverse effect on both you and the person you are taking care of.

There are various ways available to control anger as a caregiver. Seeking help from family members, friends, or a professional counselor is one option. Engaging in stress reducing activities, e.g. meditation or exercise, setting practical expectations for yourself and others, and discovering ways to take a break and prioritize your own needs are all great techniques. Additionally, it is important to have open and honest communication with the person you are caring for and involve them in decision-making regarding their care.

Causes of Anger in Full-Time Caregivers

Full-time caregiving can be overwhelming, and caregivers often take on more responsibilities than they can handle. This overload of responsibilities can lead to feelings of frustration and anger. Lack of support is also a major cause of anger in full-time caregivers. Caregiving is often an isolating experience, and caregivers may feel unsupported and unappreciated. Additionally, emotional exhaustion, mental strain and physical exhaustion are common causes of anger in full-time caregivers.

"CAREGIVING CAN BE AN OVERWHELMING AND EXHAUSTING EXPERIENCE... "

Thanksgiving In June

Millicent had always looked up to her Uncle Richard. He had been her hero since she was young, always there for her, providing guidance, and offering a helping hand. That's why when he needed her, she didn't hesitate to become his caregiver. She moved him into her small apartment, allowing him to bring his beloved cat, Joshua, and made sure he was well taken care of. However, as time went on, Millicent realized that being a caregiver was not always easy, especially when someone you love is no longer the same person they used to be.

Initially, things went well but as time passed, Richard's condition started deteriorating. He began to forget things and make mistakes. This came as a surprise to Millie, as

43

he had always been regarded as highly intelligent and organized.

Now, her hero was failing, leaving her feeling bewildered and disappointed.

One day, in June, when Millicent came home from work, after staying late to make some overtime, she found that Richard had taken all the food out of the freezer and had cooked almost all of it. He had also put the hamburger in the oven without removing it from the Styrofoam container creating a mess inside. Millicent was livid; she yelled, flailed her arms, stomped around the kitchen and dumped the poorly cooked food into the trash. "Why did you cook all the food Uncle Richard? What were you trying to do?", she screamed at the top of her lungs. Richard stared blankly and asked why she was so angry. After all, he was just trying to earn his keep and help her with Thanksgiving dinner. He didn't realize it was only June.

Millicent was at a loss for what to do. The man she had always admired for his intelligence was failing her. She felt bewildered and disappointed. She had to remind herself that it wasn't Richard's fault - he was struggling with old age, and it was her job to take care of him.

"I'm sorry, Unc," Millicent said as she tried to compose herself. "I appreciate your efforts, but we can't eat this. It's not cooked properly."

Richard nodded, looking down at the floor.

"I know I'm not the same person I used to be, Millie," Richard said, his voice shaking. "I feel like a burden on you, and I don't like it."

Millicent's heart ached as she realized just how much her uncle was struggling. She took a deep breath and placed both hands on Richard's shoulders, looking into his eyes. "You're not a burden, Uncle Richard," said

Millicent. "I love you, and I'm doing this because I want to. You took care of me when I was young, and now it's my turn to take care of you."

Richard looked up at Millicent, his eyes glistening with tears.

"You're a good woman, Millie," said Richard. "I'm lucky to have you in my life."

But for Millie, it wasn't just about the food. It was about the frustration and fear that came with being a caregiver. She was overwhelmed with the responsibility of taking care of Richard and the added burden of having to teach him everything from scratch. It felt like the weight of the world was on her shoulders.

But this incident turned out to be a turning point for both of them. Millie realized that anger wasn't going to help and that she had to be patient and kind to him. She began explaining things in simple terms and taught him step-by-step how to cook. She even bought him a cookbook with easy-to-follow recipes and they started cooking together.

Millicent was reminded that being a caregiver is not just about physically taking care of someone; it's also about taking care of them. It's a full-time job that requires patience, understanding, and compassion. It's not always easy, but it's worth it to help someone you love.

Millicent realized that her uncle may not be able to do things the way he used to, but that didn't mean he had lost his intelligence or worth. She decided to approach caregiving with empathy and positivity, and she and Richard grew closer than ever before.

Caring for a loved one can be difficult, but it's also an opportunity to show kindness and compassion. Sometimes, it's easy to forget that the person you're caring for may be struggling emotionally, and it's important to be patient and understanding. Millicent learned this lesson the hard way, but she grew closer to her uncle in the process. In the end, caregiving proved to be a rewarding and meaningful experience for both Millicent and Richard.

As a result, their relationship grew stronger, and Richard's condition improved. He started to remember things and take better care of himself. Millie was overjoyed to see the positive changes and appreciated the moments they spent together.

Being a caregiver is never easy. It requires patience, compassion, and a lot of sacrifice. But it's also a journey filled with lessons and redemption. As Millie discovered, taking care of someone you love means learning to understand their limitations, and most importantly, learning to love them unconditionally, even in the face of mistakes.

The experience taught her to be strong, be patient, and to never give up on someone she loves.

Effects of Anger on Full-Time Caregivers

Anger can have serious effects on full-time caregivers. Caregivers who frequently experience anger are at risk for a number of health problems, such as high blood pressure, heart disease, and depression.

Additionally, their interpersonal relationships may suffer as well, as they tend to become irritable and withdraw from their loved ones.

Signs of Anger in Full-Time Caregivers

It is important to recognize the signs of anger in full-time caregivers, as early intervention can prevent harmful consequences. Physical symptoms of anger may include headaches, muscle tension, and stomach problems. Emotional symptoms can manifest as feeling overwhelmed, irritable, or easily frustrated. Behavioral symptoms include yelling, arguing, or becoming physically aggressive.

Overcoming Anger in Full-Time Caregivers

Caregivers who are experiencing anger should seek professional help, such as therapy or counseling. Joining support groups with other caregivers can also be beneficial. Practicing self-care is essential for caregivers, and taking time to engage in activities they enjoy can help reduce anger. Caregivers should not be afraid to ask for help from friends and family.

Results Over Time

Overcoming anger in full-time caregivers can have positive long-term effects. Caregivers who have learned to manage their anger report improved emotional and physical well-being, better quality of care for their loved ones, and strengthened interpersonal relationships. Seeking help and learning to cope with anger can lead to a more fulfilling caregiving experience.

How to Handle Anger in Full-Time Caregivers

Handling anger in full-time caregivers requires managing expectations, setting boundaries, and practicing relaxation techniques. Caregivers should have realistic expectations of themselves and their loved ones and learn to ask for help when necessary. Setting boundaries for personal time and space can also help prevent feelings of anger. Relaxation techniques such as deep breathing, meditation, and yoga can help caregivers manage their emotions.

Finally, full-time caregivers may experience feelings of anger and frustration, but there are ways to overcome these emotions.

Seeking professional help, practicing self-care, and managing expectations can all help caregivers manage anger and improve their quality of life.

Frequently Asked Questions: (FAQs)

Can anger in full-time caregivers harm the care recipient?

Anger can negatively impact the care recipient's well-being and can increase the risk of burnout for caregivers.

What are some relaxation techniques that caregivers can use to manage anger?

Deep breathing, meditation, and yoga are all effective relaxation techniques.

How can caregivers ask for help from friends and family?

Caregivers should be honest about their needs and communicate clearly with loved ones about how they can help.

Can therapy or counseling really help caregivers overcome anger?

Yes, therapy or counseling can be a valuable tool for caregivers who are struggling with anger and other emotions.

Is it normal to feel angry as a full-time caregiver?

It is normal to experience a range of emotions as a caregiver, including anger. Seeking help and support can help manage these emotions.

"CAREGIVERS MAY FEEL SOCIALLY ISOLATED..."

ANXIETY

Anxiety is a common emotion experienced by many people, including full-time caregivers. It is characterized by feelings of unease, apprehension, or worry, often accompanied by physical sensations such as sweating, trembling, or an increased heart rate.

For full-time caregivers, anxiety may be related to the stress and demands of providing care to a loved one who is ill, disabled, or elderly. Caregivers may experience anxiety about their ability to provide adequate care, concerns about the health and well-being of their loved one, financial pressures, or social isolation.

Anxiety is a common experience for caregivers, as caregiving can be a challenging and sometimes overwhelming responsibility.

Here are some ways that anxiety can present itself in caregiving:

Physical symptoms: Anxiety can manifest in physical symptoms such as fatigue, headaches, muscle tension, and trouble sleeping.

Constant worry: Caregivers may worry about the health and safety of their loved one, financial concerns, and the future.

Feeling overwhelmed: Caregivers may feel like there is too much to do and not enough time to do it, leading to feelings of overwhelm and stress.

Guilt: Caregivers may feel guilty if they take time for themselves or if they feel like they are not doing enough.

Social isolation: Caregivers may feel socially isolated if they are unable to participate in social activities or if they feel like they cannot leave their loved one alone.

Some strategies for managing anxiety in caregiving include:

Seeking support: Talking to friends, family members, or a therapist can help caregivers manage their anxiety and stress.

Taking breaks: Caregivers should take time for themselves to engage in activities they enjoy, such as reading, exercising, or spending time with friends.

Prioritizing tasks: Caregivers should prioritize tasks and consider delegating tasks to others when possible.

Learning relaxation techniques: Deep breathing, meditation, and progressive muscle relaxation can help caregivers manage stress and anxiety.

Practicing self-care: Caregivers should make sure they are taking care of their physical and emotional needs, including eating well, getting enough sleep, and engaging in self-care activities.

"CAREGIVERS WHO ARE EXPERIENCING ANXIETY MAY FIND IT MORE CHALLENGING TO PROVIDE CARE EFFECTIVELY."

Wrestling with Anxiety

Rashidi had always prided himself on being a cool, collected guy. He had spent years mastering martial arts and becoming an expert marksman at the gun range, and he had earned a master's degree in psychology from Villanova University. He had faced many challenges in his life, but nothing could have prepared him for what was about to come.

One day, his wife Ramona was involved in a horrific car accident that left her paralyzed from the waist down and terribly traumatized. Rashidi was devastated by the news, but he knew he had to be strong for his wife and their four children, who ranged in age from 8 to 14.

For the first few days after the accident, Rashidi felt like he was in a daze. He struggled to come to terms with the fact that his wife, who had always been so full of life and energy, was now confined to a wheelchair. He felt overwhelmed by the responsibility of caring for her and their children, who were all struggling to deal with the aftermath of the accident.

51

As the weeks and months went by, Rashidi's anxiety began to mount. He found himself constantly worried about his wife's physical and emotional well-being, as well as the impact that her accident was having on their children. He felt like he was always on edge, waiting for something else to go wrong.

Moreover, Rashidi was also dealing with the pressures of his teaching position at Central High School. He had always been a dedicated and passionate teacher, but now he found himself struggling to keep up with his workload while also caring for his family. He felt like he was constantly juggling multiple responsibilities and never had a moment to himself.

The anxiety began to take a toll on Rashidi's physical and mental health. He found himself struggling to sleep at night, and he began to experience panic attacks during the day. He tried to put on a brave face for his family and his colleagues at work, but inside he was falling apart.

Eventually, Rashidi realized that he needed help. He began seeing a therapist who specialized in helping caregivers cope with the stress and anxiety of caring for a loved one. He also started taking medication to help manage his symptoms.

Over time, Rashidi learned how to better manage his anxiety. He found ways to carve out time for himself, whether it was going for a run in the morning or taking a few minutes to meditate during his lunch break. He also learned how to ask for help when he needed it, whether it was from friends, family, or his colleagues at work.

It wasn't easy, but eventually Rashidi and his family found a new normal. They learned how to navigate the challenges of life with a family member who had a disability, and as a result, they grew closer. Rashidi still struggled with anxiety from time to time, but he knew that he had the tools and support he needed to get through it.

Being a caregiver can be demanding and anxiety can have a significant impact on a caregiver's physical and emotional well-being.

Here are some ways anxiety can affect a caregiver:

Physical symptoms: Anxiety can cause physical symptoms such as headaches, muscle tension, fatigue, upset stomach, and difficulty sleeping. These symptoms can make it more challenging to provide care effectively and can reduce the overall quality of life for the caregiver.

Emotional distress: Caregivers can experience a range of emotions, including sadness, anger, frustration, guilt, and helplessness. Anxiety can intensify these emotions and make it difficult for caregivers to manage their feelings in a healthy way.

Decreased ability to provide care: Caregivers who are experiencing anxiety may find it more challenging to provide care effectively. They may have difficulty focusing, making decisions, and carrying out tasks efficiently, which can negatively impact the person they are caring for.

Increased risk of burnout: Caregiver burnout is a state of physical, emotional, and mental exhaustion that can occur when caregivers experience chronic stress and feel overwhelmed by their caregiving responsibilities. Anxiety can increase the risk of burnout, as caregivers may struggle to manage their stress levels effectively.

Overall, anxiety can have a significant impact on a caregiver's ability to provide care effectively. It's essential for caregivers to prioritize their own self-care and seek support when needed to manage their anxiety and maintain their well-being.

Frequently Asked Questions: (FAQs)

What are some common causes of anxiety in full-time caregivers?

Increased responsibility and commitment, financial strain, lack of support and social isolation, and high expectations.

How does anxiety affect full-time caregivers?

Anxiety can cause physical and emotional symptoms, increase the risk of health problems, and negatively affect efficacy in caregiving roles.

How can full-time caregivers manage their anxiety?

They can practice self-care and stress management, seek support and help, and set realistic expectations for themselves.

Can caregivers experience positive results over time with the management of anxiety?

Yes, caregivers can experience better physical and emotional health, reduced stress levels, and improved caregiving roles with consistent self-care and supportive strategies.

Where can caregivers access resources and support for managing anxiety?

Caregivers can find resources and support through family, friends, healthcare providers, counseling/therapy services, and networks with fellow caregivers.

DEPRESSION

The feeling of being depressed can be defined as a persistent feeling of sadness or loss of interest in activities that one used to enjoy, along with other symptoms such as changes in sleep patterns, changes in appetite, feelings of worthlessness or guilt, difficulty concentrating, and thoughts of death or suicide.

For full-time caregivers, the feeling of being depressed can also be accompanied by feelings of overwhelm, exhaustion, and isolation. Caregiving can be a demanding and stressful role, and caregivers can often feel like they are putting their own needs aside to care for someone else. This can lead to feelings of burnout and depression.

Depression can affect people of all ages, genders, and backgrounds. It is a serious condition that can have a significant impact on an individual's quality of life, relationships, and ability to function in daily activities. Depression can also cause physical and psychological symptoms including changes in appetite, sleep disturbances, fatigue, aches and pains, difficulty concentrating, and feelings of worthlessness or guilt.

It is a serious condition that can have a significant impact on a person's quality of life.

"DEPRESSION CAN WEAKEN THE IMMUNE SYSTEM"

There are several types of depression, including major depressive disorder, persistent depressive disorder, seasonal affective disorder, and postpartum depression. Treatment for depression typically involves a combination of medication, therapy, lifestyle changes, or a combination of all.

Now, let's delve into a story about Anita who is caring for her fifteen-year-old daughter Roseanne:

Defeating Depression

Anita is a loving, caring mother to Roseanne, who has been diagnosed with a chronic illness that necessitates constinous medical care and attention. Consequently, Anita had willingly and thoughtfully assumed the role of being Roseanne's primary caregiver.

At first, Anita was able to handle the demands of caring for her daughter. She was determined to do everything she could to help Roseanne manage her illness and provide her with the best possible care. However, as time went on, Anita began to feel increasingly overwhelmed and isolated.

Anita's days were consumed with managing Roseanne's medical appointments, administering medications, and ensuring that she was eating a healthy diet. She often had to juggle these responsibilities with her job and other household chores. She began to feel like she had no time for herself, and her own health and well-being began to suffer.

Despite her best efforts, Roseanne's health continued to deteriorate. Anita felt helpless and was consumed by feelings of guilt and inadequacy. She began to withdraw from her friends and family, and her once-bright outlook on life began to darken.

As the weeks turned into months, Anita's depression deepened. She struggled to find joy in anything and felt like she was failing both as a caregiver and as a mother. She was convinced that she was letting her daughter down and felt like she had no one to turn to for support.

Eventually, Anita realized that she needed help. She reached out to a therapist who specialized in working with caregivers of children with chronic illnesses. Through therapy, Anita was able to process her feelings of guilt and inadequacy and develop strategies for coping with the demands of caregiving.

With time, Anita began to feel more hopeful and optimistic about the future. She learned to prioritize her own needs and to ask for help when she needed it. She also began to see that despite the challenges, caring for

> Roseanne was a source of great meaning and purpose in her life.
>
> In the end, Anita emerged from her depression stronger and more resilient than ever before. She continued to care for Roseanne with love and dedication, but also with a newfound sense of self-compassion and perspective.

Depression can have a number of negative effects on a caregiver, particularly if they are caring for someone with a chronic illness or disability.

"TALK TO A THERAPIST, COUNSELOR, OR SUPPORT GROUP"

Some potential effects of depression on a caregiver include:

Increased stress and anxiety: Depression can make it more difficult for a caregiver to manage their own stress and anxiety levels, which may already be high due to the demands of caregiving.

Reduced quality of life: Caregiving can be emotionally and physically draining. Depression can make it more difficult for a caregiver to find joy in their daily life and may lead to feelings of isolation and loneliness.

Physical health problems: Depression can weaken the immune system and increase the risk of developing physical health problems, such as chronic pain, heart disease, and diabetes. Caregivers who are already at risk for these conditions may be more vulnerable to their effects.

Reduced ability to provide care: If a caregiver is struggling with depression, they may have less energy and motivation to provide the level of care that their loved one needs.

Increased risk of burnout: Caregivers who are struggling with depression may be more likely to experience burnout, which can lead to feelings of exhaustion, frustration, and resentment.

It is not uncommon for caregivers to experience feelings of depression especially if they are providing care for a loved one with a chronic or terminal illness.

Overall, depression can have a significant impact on a caregiver to provide effective care and maintain their own physical and emotional well-being. It is important for caregivers to seek support and treatment if they are struggling with depression.

Here are some tips that may help if you are feeling depressed while caregiving:

Take care of yourself: It's important to prioritize your own physical and emotional well-being. Make sure you are getting enough sleep, eating a healthy diet, and exercising regularly.

Seek support: Talk to a therapist, counselor, or support group to help you cope with your feelings. It can be helpful to speak with someone who understands what you are going through and can offer guidance.

Set boundaries: It's important to set boundaries and prioritize your own needs. Don't be afraid to ask for help, delegate tasks, or take breaks when you need them.

Practice self-care: Engage in activities that you enjoy and that help you relax, such as reading, listening to music, or taking a bath. Make time for yourself, even if it's just a few minutes a day.

Seek professional help: If your feelings of depression persist or become overwhelming, it may be helpful to speak with a mental health professional. They can provide you with additional resources and support.

Remember, it's important to take care of yourself so that you can continue to provide the best care possible to your loved one.

Frequently Asked Questions: (FAQs)

What are some common causes of depression in caregivers?

Giving up a career or social life, lack of support, and financial pressure are some common causes of depression in caregivers.

Can taking care of a loved one cause depression?

Yes, taking care of a loved one can lead to depression, especially if the caregiver feels overwhelmed, isolated, and unsupported.

What are some self-care strategies for caregivers dealing with depression?

Self-care strategies for caregivers dealing with depression include regular exercise, eating healthy, getting enough sleep, and practicing mindfulness.

Is it common for full-time caregivers to feel isolated and overwhelmed?

Yes, it's common for full-time caregivers to feel isolated and overwhelmed, given the challenging demands of caregiving.

When is it best to seek professional help for depression as a caregiver?

Caregivers should seek professional help for depression as soon as possible if they experience suicidal ideation, loss of interest in activities, difficulty in taking care of themselves and the people they are caring for, or if their depression is affecting their daily functioning.

Exhaustion

Caregiver exhaustion, also known as burnout is a state of physical, emotional and mental exhaustion. It may be accompanied by a change in attitude, from positive and caring to negative and unconcerned. Burnout can occur when caregivers do not receive the necessary help or when they attempt to do more than they are capable of both physically or financially.

Many caregivers also feel guilty if they spend time on themselves rather than on their ill or elderly loved ones. Caregivers who experience "burn out" may suffer from fatigue, stress, anxiety and depression.

Exhaustion is a common experience among full-time caregivers and can have significant negative effects on both the caregiver and the person receiving care. Caregiver exhaustion can lead to physical, emotional, and psychological distress and has long-term implications for the wellbeing of the caregiver. Therefore, it's crucial to understand the causes, signs, and methods of overcoming exhaustion to ensure adequate care for both the caregiver and the person they are caring for.

"BURNOUT CAN OCCUR
WHEN CAREGIVERS
DON'T GET THE HELP THEY NEED."

Causes of exhaustion in caregivers may include:

Over commitment: Many full-time caregivers take on too much responsibility, leading to a sense of being overwhelmed or overburdened.

Lack of Support: Caregiving in isolation can lead to feelings of loneliness and frustration.

Financial Strain: The financial burden of caregiving can place significant stress on caregivers and contribute to exhaustion.

Loss of Identity: Caregiving can often consume a person's identity, leading to a loss of self and exacerbating feelings of exhaustion.

The effects of exhaustion on full-time caregivers can be serious and can include:

Physical Health Problems: Caregivers who suffer from exhaustion may experience physical symptoms such as headaches, muscle tension, and an increased susceptibility to illness.

Emotional Distress: Exhaustion can lead to emotional difficulties such as depression, anxiety, anger, and irritability.

Relationship Strain: Caregiver exhaustion can strain the caregiver's relationships with the person they are caring for, family members, and friends.

Some signs that a caregiver may be experiencing exhaustion include:

- Chronic fatigue
- Increased irritability or mood swings
- Difficulty concentrating or making decisions
- Neglecting one's own health and well-being
- Social withdrawal and isolation
- Increased use of drugs or alcohol
- Decreased interest in hobbies or activities

"CAREGIVERS MAY FEEL DEFEATED."

Overcoming exhaustion requires a multi-faceted approach, including:

- Seeking and accepting help from others
- Taking regular breaks and time for self-care
- Seeking counseling or support groups
- Prioritizing healthy habits such as exercise, nutrition, and sleep
- Finding ways to reduce stress and increase relaxation
- Engaging in activities that bring joy and fulfillment
- Setting realistic expectations and boundaries

The Tired Twin

Barbara had always been close to her twin sister Brenda. They had been inseparable since childhood and had shared everything. So when Brenda suffered a heart attack and stroke, Barbara knew that she had to step up and take care of her sister.

Being the primary caregiver wasn't easy for Brenda She needed a lot of hands-on care, and being fairly overweight with diabetes meant that she required a special diet. Barbara was constantly worried about not following doctors' orders and adding more stress to her already overworked schedule.

One day, while assisting Brenda with her physical therapy exercises, Barbara couldn't help expressing her concerns. "Brenda, I'm really worried that I'm not doing enough to take care of you. I feel like I'm not following the doctor's orders and it's adding more stress to my already busy schedule."

Brenda looked up at Barbara with a worried expression on her face. "I know it's hard, Barbara. But you're doing the best you can. I appreciate everything you're doing for me," she said.

Barbara let out a deep sigh and sat down next to Brenda. "I just wish there was a better solution. I'm exhausted, and I don't know how much longer I can keep this up."

Brenda thought for a moment before speaking. "What if we hired a professional caregiver? Someone who could help you with my care and take some of the burden off your shoulders?"

Barbara's eyes lit up at the suggestion. "That's a great idea! I don't know why I didn't think of it before. It would definitely make things easier for both of us."

With that, Brenda and Barbara decided to look into hiring a professional caregiver. They found someone who was experienced in caring for patients with similar conditions as Brenda and who could provide the extra help that Barbara needed.

The new caregiver quickly became a part of the family, and Barbara finally had the time to take care of herself and her own needs. Brenda's health improved, and Barbara's stress levels decreased significantly.

In the end, Barbara realized that being a caregiver didn't mean she had to do everything alone. Sometimes, the best solution was to reach out for help and find the support she needed to take care of her loved ones while also taking care of herself.

The results of overcoming exhaustion can be significant, including:

- Improved physical and emotional health

- Increased energy and motivation

- Greater sense of purpose and fulfillment

- Improved relationships with loved ones

- Increased ability to provide quality care to the person being cared for

Exhaustion is a common experience among full-time caregivers that can have significant negative effects on both caregivers and the person they are caring for. It's crucial to understand the causes, signs, and methods of overcoming exhaustion to ensure adequate care for both parties. Caregivers should be encouraged to seek support, engage in self-care, and delegate tasks to prevent long-term negative effects.

Frequently Asked Questions: (FAQs)

What is caregiver burnout?

Caregiver burnout is a state of physical, emotional, and mental exhaustion that occurs when a caregiver is overwhelmed by the demands of caring for someone else.

How common is caregiver exhaustion?

Caregiver exhaustion is a common experience among full-time caregivers, with approximately 40-70% of caregivers reporting that they feel overwhelmed or overburdened.

What are some ways to prevent caregiver exhaustion?

Some ways to prevent caregiver exhaustion include taking regular breaks, seeking and accepting help from others, prioritizing self-care, and finding ways to reduce stress.

How can family members support a full-time caregiver?

Family members can support a full-time caregiver by offering help with caregiving tasks, providing emotional support, and ensuring the caregiver has regular breaks and time for self-care.

Can caregiver exhaustion lead to chronic illness?

Prolonged caregiver exhaustion can lead to the development of chronic health conditions such as heart disease, diabetes, and hypertension.

Is it possible to experience caregiver exhaustion and not know it?

Yes, many caregivers may not recognize that they are experiencing exhaustion or may believe that it's just a normal part of the caregiving experience.

FEAR

Fear is a common emotion experienced by many caregivers, especially those who care for individuals with chronic illnesses, disabilities, or other medical conditions.

Fear can be defined as an emotional response to a perceived threat or danger. In the case of caregivers, fear may arise from concerns about the health and well-being of the person they are caring for, worries about making mistakes or not being able to provide adequate care, or anxiety about the future.

Fear can also be a natural response to the stress and demands of caregiving, and it is important for caregivers to take steps to manage their fears and prioritize their own well-being in order to provide the best possible care for their loved one.

As a full-time caregiver, fear is an emotion that you may experience frequently. The fear of losing the person you are caring for, the fear of making a wrong decision or the fear of not being able to provide the necessary care are common among caregivers. On this topic we will discuss the causes, effects, signs, overcoming strategies, results over time, and how to handle the fear that full-time caregivers may experience.

Being a full-time caregiver is not an easy job. It requires physical and mental strength to carry out daily activities and management of illnesses or disabilities of the care recipient. Sometimes, the responsibility of caregiving can overburden the caregiver, creating an intense emotional experience that includes fear and anxiety.

Caregivers who do not know how to deal with fear can develop an overwhelming burden of responsibilities and stress, leading to burnout and potential health problems. Therefore, the fear of a caregiver should never be taken lightly and must be addressed to ensure the well-being of the caregiver and the care recipient.

Caregivers may be afraid of the outcome of a person's illness or disability, which may result in the person's death. The responsibility of taking care of a person's needs and ensuring their safety can be daunting, creating fear and anxiety in the caregiver.

Financial burden and lack of support are issues that caregivers may face, which lead to emotional distress and a fear of the future. Long-term care costs, medical expenses, and personal debt are often significant concerns in conservative, low-income families that can lead to fear in caregivers.

Effects of Fear on Full-Time Caregivers

Fear can negatively impact the caregivers' health and well-being. The emotional and physical stress can lead to feelings of insecurity, depression, and anxiety. Fear can also affect the quality of care provided to the care recipient, making it difficult for the caregiver to focus on the recipient's needs.

Signs of Fearful in Full-Time Caregivers

The caregivers can experience sleeplessness, depression, irritability, nervousness, and feelings of isolation, to name a few of the signs of fear when they're carrying their responsibilities. It can be challenging to express fears about caregiving, feeling shameful and as if they are failing at their job.

Dwayne's Fears - Real or Imagined?

Dwayne had always been a worrier. Even as a child, he would fret about things that others his age never even considered. As he grew older, his worries became more intense, until they sometimes led to full-blown panic attacks. But despite his struggles, Dwayne was determined to be there for his father, Raymond.

Raymond was a widower who had been diagnosed with Alzheimer's disease several years ago. Dwayne had moved in with him to provide care, but his fear of causing his father harm was sometimes overwhelming. He worried about accidentally giving him the wrong medication or forgetting to lock the door and allowing someone to break in.

Despite his fears, Dwayne did his best to care for his father. He made sure that he took his medications on time, cooked him healthy meals, and took him on walks in the park. But every time he made a mistake, no matter how small, his fear would skyrocket.

One day, Dwayne was in the kitchen preparing lunch when he suddenly felt a wave of panic wash over him. He imagined his father choking on his food or falling and hurting himself. He started to hyperventilate, and his hands began to shake. He knew he needed to calm down, but he couldn't seem to get a grip on his thoughts.

69

Just then, Raymond walked into the kitchen, looking confused and disoriented. Dwayne's panic intensified as he realized that his father was having a bad day. He struggled to keep his own fear at bay as he helped his father sit down at the table and served him his lunch.

As they ate, Dwayne tried to focus on his father's needs instead of his own fears. He asked him about his day and listened patiently as he struggled to remember the details. He offered him encouragement and support, even as his own anxiety threatened to overwhelm him.

Slowly but surely, Dwayne began to feel his fear subside. He realized that his father needed him, and that his love for him was stronger than his fear of making a mistake. He took a deep breath and promised himself that he would do everything in his power to give his father the care he so desperately needed.

"ADOPT STRESS-RELIEVING ACTIVITIES THAT' EMPOWER POSITIVE EMOTIONS AND PUSH AWAY NEGATIVE FEELINGS."

From that day forward, Dwayne worked hard to overcome his fear. He sought therapy and learned coping strategies to help him manage his anxiety. He made sure to take breaks and practice self-care so that he could be a better caregiver for his father.

In the end, Dwayne learned that while his fears were real, they didn't have to control his life. He found the strength to overcome them and to be there for his father, no matter what challenges they faced. And Raymond, for his part, knew that his son loved him and was doing everything he could to care for him. Together, they faced the future with hope and determination, knowing that they could conquer anything as long as they had each other.

Overcoming Fearful Emotion in Full-Time Caregivers

Self-Care and Mental Health Treatment

Self-care is the foundation of overcoming fear in caregivers. A healthy lifestyle routine, such as healthy eating and exercise, can improve physical and emotional wellness. Engage in meditation, deep breathing, and other mindfulness techniques, to promote mental acuity. The counseling expertise from a mental health practitioner would also be beneficial for managing emotional stress.

Seeking Support from Professionals and Family

Acceptance from family and close friends enhances the strength of the caregiver. Seeking advocacy and getting support groups can lift off the burden of caring for the patient alone. Professionals, including nurse assistants and social workers, can recommend and provide additional support services that ease the caregiver's burden.

Releasing Negative Thoughts and Emotions

The fear of being a caregiver may have a negative effect on your mental well-being. It is crucial to remind yourself that you're doing your best and have done all that you could. Adopt stress-relieving activities that' empower positive emotions and push away negative feelings.

Results over Time When Overcoming Fearful Emotion

With consistent self-care, support from family and friends, and other stress-relieving techniques, caregivers can significantly decrease the feeling of fear and anxiety. Positive results include less stress, increased self-confidence, improved mental and physical wellness, and better quality of care for the recipient.

How to Handle Fearful Emotion Meditation and Mindful Breathing Techniques

Several mindfulness techniques can be used to relieve stress and anxiety in caregivers, which include meditation and mindful breathing. These practices are useful in reducing the heart rate and promoting breathing regulation, which helps one feel relaxed and helps maintain a positive mental attitude.

Counseling and Support Groups

Professional counseling and support groups are excellent tools for caregivers, allowing them to engage with their peers and share experiences of caring for their loved ones. Participating in support groups or counseling can inspire new strategies and techniques for overcoming fear.

Identifying Triggers and Coping Strategies

By identifying the source of fear, caregivers can avoid triggers that cause them. Part of that entails having a plan of emotional intervention to help them cope with the situation. Successful strategies include thoughts focusing on personal growth, self-appreciation affirmations, and practical approaches that allow individuals to stay focused on their objectives.

In conclusion, the role of a full-time caregiver is a phenomenal, challenging responsibility, with many unique stressors and burdens. Fear is a natural emotion that one may experience, but it is not something that one should take lightly. To avoid experiencing burnout and other health complications, caregivers need to adopt effective coping mechanisms and continue to provide the best possible care for the care recipient.

Frequently Asked Questions: (FAQ's)

How common is it for full-time caregivers to experience fear?

Many caregivers experience fear in many forms. Fear usually develops when a caregiver feels overwhelmed with responsibility, resulting in emotional distress.

Should a caregiver speak with a mental health expert when dealing with fear?

Yes, it is always wise to speak with mental health expert or professional to cope and address emotional stress effectively.

What should I do when fear starts to take over my thoughts?

One can use a relaxation technique, breathing exercises, or mindfulness mediation to help calm fear and provide a clear-minded approach.

What should I do when fear persists despite my efforts?

Engage or speak with support groups, friends, and close family members. Alternatively, try to adopt an alternative coping mechanism that will mitigate or explore new ways to tackle the situation.

How do I know if my caregiver job is causing many fears?

If you are experiencing sleeplessness, depression, irritability, nervousness, and feelings of isolation, it's possible that you are carrying the load of caregiver responsibility.

"CAREGIVING: THE JOY OF MAKING A DIFFERENCE."

FRUSTRATION

Frustration in full-time caregivers refers to the feelings of dissatisfaction, exasperation, and emotional strain experienced by individuals who are responsible for providing continuous care and support to another person. Full-time caregivers often face significant challenges, including the physical and emotional demands of caregiving, the loss of personal time and freedom, financial burdens, and the potential for burnout.

As the number of the aging population increases, there is a growing need for fulltime caregivers. These caregivers are responsible for providing long term care to individuals who require assistance with their daily activities due to chronic illnesses or disabilities. However, being a full-time caregiver can be overwhelming and often leads to frustration. If not addressed in a timely manner, this frustration can become chronic and result in burnout. This topic will discuss the causes, effects, signs, and strategies for overcoming frustration in full-time caregivers.

75

Causes of Frustration in Full-Time Caregivers

Heavy Workload: Full-time caregivers often have to attend to the needs of their care receivers round the clock, which means they cannot take a break whenever they want. The heavy workload can become overwhelming, leading to frustration.

"CAREGIVING CAN BE A FULL-TIME JOB."

Personal Issues: Caregivers may have personal problems, that can make it even harder for them to cope with caregiving. Personal problems, such as marital issues, financial struggles, or health concerns can lead to frustration and eventually burnout.

Financial Issues: Caregiving can be a full-time job, and any caregivers sacrifice their paid employment to provide care for their loved ones. This can lead to financial strain, especially when the caregiver is the sole provider for the family.

Lack of Support: Caregiving can become less overwhelming when the caregiver receives support from family, friends, or professional organizations. However, a lack of support can lead to frustration.

Lack of Knowledge: Some caregivers may not have the necessary skills and knowledge to provide proper care. This can make caregiving more demanding and frustrating.

Medical Conditions of the Care Receiver: The medical condition of the person receiving care can also contribute to frustration. Conditions such as dementia or Alzheimer's can lead to aggressive behavior, which can be challenging and frustrating for the caregiver.

Effects of Frustration in Full-Time Caregivers
Frustration can lead to various negative effects, including:

- Emotional exhaustion
- Depression
- Anxiety
- Irritability
- Physical exhaustion
- Social isolation
- Health issues such as hypertension and heart diseases.

Signs of Frustration in Full-Time Caregivers
Physical Signs

- Frequent headaches
- Fatigue
- Insomnia
- Loss of appetite
- Weight gain or loss
- Frequent colds or flu
- Digestive problems such as stomach ulcers

Emotional Signs

- Anxiety
- Depression
- Irritability
- Resentment
- Guilt

- Hopelessness

- Anger

- Mood swings

Behavioral Signs

- Neglecting personal hygiene

- Drug or alcohol abuse

- Social withdrawal

- Carelessness

- Aggressive behavior

- Poor judgment

The Boiling Point of Frustration

Pamela had always been a woman who took charge of her life. She was a successful businesswoman who lived life on her own terms. However, when her mother Jean's dementia started progressing, Pamela knew that she had to move in with her mother to take care of her.

At first, Pamela thought she could handle everything. She believed she had the patience to deal with her mother's illogical decisions, losing things, and being uncooperative. However, as time passed, Pamela found herself becoming increasingly frustrated.

"Pam, where did you put my purse?" Jean asked one day, looking around the room.

"I didn't touch your purse, Mom. You probably left it somewhere," Pamela replied, trying to remain calm.

"I always keep it on the table next to my bed. You moved it," Jean insisted.

"I didn't move it, Mom. Please try to remember where you put it," Pamela said, her voice starting to rise.

"I don't know where it is. You're supposed to help me," Jean said, tears welling up in her eyes.

"I am helping you, Mom. But you have to understand that I can't keep track of everything all the time," Pamela said, feeling her frustration boiling over.

Another time, Jean refused to take her medication, insisting that she didn't need it. Pamela tried to reason with her, but Jean was stubborn and uncooperative.

"Mom, you have to take your medication. It's important for your health," Pamela said.

"I don't want to take it. It makes me feel sick," Jean replied.

"It's not supposed to make you feel sick, Mom. It's supposed to help you," Pamela said, her voice tinged with irritation.

"I don't care. I'm not taking it," Jean said, crossing her arms.

Pamela felt like she was at her wit's end. Her frustration was affecting her mental and physical health. She started drinking more frequently, hoping to find some relief from the stress. But it only made things worse. She even started experimenting with cocaine, which was a dangerous path to go down.

Eventually, Pamela realized that she needed help. She couldn't do this alone. She reached out to support groups and found a caregiver who could help her take care of her mother. With some help, Pamela was able to take care of her mother and take care of herself too. She started eating healthy, going for walks, and took up painting as a hobby.

It wasn't easy, but with some help, Pamela was able to find a balance between taking care of her mother and taking care of herself. She learned that self-care was just as important as caring for others, especially when you're a primary caregiver.

Overcoming Strategies for Frustration in Full-Time Caregivers

Self-Care

Caregivers should take care of their physical, emotional, and spiritual well-being. They can take breaks, practice relaxation techniques such as yoga or meditation, and maintain healthy eating habits and exercise routines.

Seek Professional Help

Caregivers can seek professional help from healthcare professionals or support groups to manage their stress and frustration. Counselors or therapists can help caregivers cope with their emotions and build problem-solving skills.

Acceptance

Accepting that caregiving can be difficult and frustrating can help caregivers develop a positive attitude towards caregiving. They should acknowledge that they cannot control everything and learn to let go of things they cannot change.

Problem-Solving Skills

Caregivers can develop problem-solving skills to learn how to prioritize tasks, set realistic goals, delegate responsibilities, and find solutions to problems.

Build Support Networks

Caregivers should build support networks of family, friends, professional organizations, and support groups. They can reach out to others for help when they need it.

Get Educated about Caregiving

Caregivers can enroll in caregiving education programs to obtain the necessary skills and knowledge to provide care effectively.

Results of Overcoming Frustration in Full-Time Caregivers

Overcoming frustration can lead to positive outcomes, including:

- Enhanced ability to provide quality care
- Improved physical, emotional, and spiritual well-being
- Better problem-solving and decision-making skills
- Better relationships with the care receiver
- Better coping skills
- Better work-life balance
- Reduced risk of burnout

Finally, frustration is a common emotion among full-time caregivers, and if not addressed timely, it can lead to burnout and other negative effects. Caregivers can overcome frustration by taking care of themselves, seeking professional help, accepting their limitations, developing problem-solving skills, building support networks, and getting educated about caregiving. Overcoming frustration can lead to better physical, emotional, and spiritual well-being, improved relationships with care receivers, better problem-solving skills, and better work-life balance.

Frequently Asked Questions: (FAQ's)

How can family members support full-time caregivers?

Family members can offer to assist with caregiving tasks, provide emotional and financial support, or offer respite care to the caregiver when they need a break.

What are some self-care tips for full-time caregivers?

Self-care tips include taking breaks, practicing relaxation techniques such as yoga or meditation, maintaining healthy eating habits and exercise routines, and seeking professional help when needed.

"CAREGIVERS CAN OVERCOME
FRUSTRATION
BY TAKING CARE OF THEMSELVES."

How can caregivers deal with aggressive behavior from care receivers?

Caregivers can seek professional help in managing aggressive behavior, develop calm and assertive communication skills, maintain a safe environment, and learn to manage their emotions.

What is the risk of burnout in full-time caregivers?

The risk of burnout is high in full-time caregivers due to the heavy workload, stress, and frustration associated with caregiving.

Can full-time caregivers obtain financial assistance?

Full-time caregivers can obtain financial assistance from government-funded programs such as Medicaid, Medicare, or local programs that offer financial aid to caregivers.

GRIEF

Grief in a full-time caregiver is a complex emotional response to the loss and changes that can accompany caring for a loved one who is chronically ill, disabled, or dying. Caregivers may experience grief as they witness the decline of their loved one's health, as they manage the demands of caregiving, and as they confront the uncertainties and challenges of providing care.

Grief can take many forms for full-time caregivers, including feelings of sadness, anger, guilt, fear, and frustration. Caregivers may also experience a sense of isolation or loneliness, as the demands of caregiving can make it difficult to maintain social connections or engage in activities that provide emotional support.

The Effects of Grief

Long-term grief can have a significant impact on caregivers who provide emotional and physical support to a loved one who is experiencing loss. Here are some of the effects of long-term grief on caregivers:

Emotional distress: Grief can cause intense emotional distress, including feelings of sadness, anger, guilt, and helplessness. Caregivers may experience these emotions themselves, or they may be affected by the emotions of the person they are caring for.

Physical symptoms: Grief can also cause physical symptoms such as fatigue, insomnia, loss of appetite, and headaches. Caregivers who are experiencing grief may struggle to take care of their own physical needs, which can lead to further health problems.

Social isolation: Caregivers may become socially isolated as they spend more time caring for their loved one and less time engaging in activities and relationships outside of their caregiving role.

Financial strain: Grief can also have financial consequences, particularly if the person being cared for had significant medical expenses or was the primary breadwinner in the household. Caregivers may need to take time off from work or reduce their hours to provide care, which can lead to a loss of income.

Burnout: Caregivers who are experiencing long-term grief may be at risk for burnout, which can manifest as physical and emotional exhaustion, cynicism, and a sense of detachment from the caregiving role.

It is important for caregivers to prioritize their own mental and physical health during the grieving process. This may involve seeking support from friends and family, joining a support group, or seeking professional counseling. Taking time for self-care activities such as exercise, meditation, or hobbies can also help caregivers manage the effects of long-term grief.

Overcome by Grief

Betty had always been a caring person. As a child, she would take in stray animals and nurse them back to health, and as an adult, she became a caregiver for the elderly and disabled. But nothing could have prepared her for the emotional journey she was about to embark on when her son Derrick was diagnosed with a rare genetic disease at the age of five.

"GRIEF AMONG FULL-TIME CAREGIVERS IS AN OFTEN OVERLOOKED TOPIC."

The first few years were hard, but Betty was determined to give her son the best care possible. She learned everything she could about the disease, attended support groups, and even started her own blog to share her experiences and connect with other parents in similar situations. She utilized her investments in order to quit her job to become a full-time caregiver, and her days were filled with doctor's appointments, physical therapy, and medication management.

Despite the challenges, Betty found joy in the small moments with her son. They would play board games, watch movies, and take walks together. Derrick was a bright and curious child, full of questions about the world around him. Betty did her best to answer them, even if she didn't always have the answers.

As years passed, Betty watched her son's condition deteriorate. He became wheelchair-bound and required a feeding tube. As his physical abilities declined, Derrick's spirit remained strong. He was always quick with a joke or a witty remark, and his smile could light up a room.

Betty's life revolved around caring for her son, and she became an expert at managing his care. She knew every medication, every dosage, and every treatment plan by heart. But despite her knowledge and dedication, she couldn't stop the disease from progressing.

When Derrick passed away at the age of 12, Betty was devastated. She had spent seven years caring for her son, and now he was gone. The grief was overwhelming, and Betty struggled to find meaning in her life without Derrick by her side.

In the weeks and months that followed, Betty found solace in her memories of Derrick. She continued to write about her experiences, and her blog became a source of comfort for others going through similar struggles. She also began volunteering at a local hospice, using her experience as a caregiver to help others in need.

"ALLOW TIME FOR GRIEVING."

Through it all, Betty never forgot the lessons she learned from her son. She learned to cherish every moment, to find joy in the small things, and to never give up hope. Though she would always carry the pain of losing her son, she knew that his memory would live on in the love and compassion she shared with others.

Overcoming Grief

Some common strategies that caregivers can use to help them cope with grief:

Seek support: It can be helpful to talk to others who have gone through similar experiences or to seek support from a therapist or counselor.

Practice self-care: Taking care of oneself is important during times of grief. This can include getting enough sleep, eating well, and engaging in regular exercise.

Engage in meaningful activities: Participating in activities that bring joy and fulfillment can help caregivers feel more positive and hopeful.

Create a memorial: Creating a memorial, such as a photo album or a scrapbook, can help caregivers keep the memory of their loved one alive.

Allow time for grieving: Grieving is a natural process, and it can take time. It is important to allow oneself to feel the full range of emotions that come with grief.

Caregivers may also experience anticipatory grief, or the sense of loss that comes with knowing that their loved one's condition will continue to deteriorate over time.

It is important to note that there is no "right" way to grieve, and everyone's experience is unique. It is important to be patient with oneself and to seek help if needed.

How to Handle Grief in Full-time Caregivers

Handling grief in full-time caregivers can be challenging, and it is essential to approach it with sensitivity. Be aware of signs of grief in yourself or others and encourage self-care and seeking support. Avoid judgment or criticism and instead, provide emotional support and offer to help with caregiving tasks.

Grief among full-time caregivers is a common but often over-looked topic. Identifying and addressing the causes and effects of grief can lead to better mental and physical health for both caregivers and care recipients. It is essential to seek support and prioritize self-care to overcome grief successfully. Full-time caregiving can be emotionally and physically exhausting, but taking care of oneself and seeking help can make the process more manageable.

Frequently Asked Questions: (FAQ's)

Is it common for full-time caregivers to experience grief?

Yes, it is common for full-time caregivers to experience grief due to the emotional attachment and stress of caregiving.

Can grief affect the physical health of full-time caregivers?

Yes, grief can lead to physical symptoms such as headaches, stomachaches, and fatigue.

What is the best way to overcome grief as a full-time caregiver?

Prioritizing self-care, seeking support, and taking breaks are effective ways to overcome grief as a full-time caregiver.

How can friends and family best support a full-time caregiver experiencing grief?

Providing emotional support, offering to help with caregiving tasks, and listening without judgment can be effective ways to support a full-time caregiver experiencing grief.

Can grief improve over time for full-time caregivers?

Yes, grief may lessen with time for full-time caregivers, but the effects may vary and never completely disappear.

GUILT

Guilt in full-time caregiving is the feeling of responsibility or remorse that arises when one believes or knows that they have done something wrong or failed to do something they should have done. It is often accompanied by feelings of shame, regret, and self-reproach. Guilt can stem from a variety of sources, including violating one's own moral code or societal norms, causing harm to others, or failing to meet personal or societal expectations.

Caregivers may feel guilty for a variety of reasons, such as feeling like they are not doing enough for their loved ones, feeling like they are not doing things correctly, feeling like they are not meeting their own expectations or the expectations of others, feeling like they are neglecting their own needs, or feeling like they are not doing enough to prevent their loved ones from experiencing pain, discomfort, or suffering.

It is important for caregivers to recognize that they are doing the best they can with the resources and support available to them, and to practice self-compassion and self-care to help manage these feelings. It can also be helpful for caregivers to seek support from other caregivers or professional resources to help them cope with the challenges of caregiving.

There are steps that caregivers can take to help alleviate these feelings and feel more confident in their role:

Acknowledge and accept your feelings: It's normal to feel guilty at times as a caregiver. Acknowledge your feelings and accept that they are a natural part of the caregiving experience.

Prioritize self-care: To be an effective caregiver, make sure you prioritize self-care activities, such as exercise, relaxation, and spending time with friends and family.

Seek support: It's important to have a support system in place, whether it's through a support group, therapist, or family and friends. Talking to others who have similar experiences can help you feel less alone and more understood.

Set realistic expectations: Caregiving can be overwhelming, and it's important to set realistic expectations for yourself and your loved one. Don't be too hard on yourself if you can't do everything, and don't feel guilty for needing to ask for help.

Celebrate your successes: It's important to recognize and celebrate your successes as a caregiver, no matter how small they may seem. Focusing on the positive can help you feel more confident and less guilty.

Remember that caregiving is a challenging role, and it's important to take care of yourself to be the best caregiver you can be.

Linda and Mary

Linda had always been close to her aunt, Mary, so, when Mary's husband passed away and she was left alone, Linda didn't hesitate to offer her a place to stay. Now, several years later, Linda had become Mary's full-time caregiver.

Linda's days were spent preparing meals, administering medication, and assisting Mary with everything from bathing to dressing. It was a difficult and exhausting job, but Linda never complained. She loved her aunt and wanted to provide her with the best care.

However, as time went on, Linda found herself growing increasingly frustrated with Mary. No matter what Linda did, it was never enough. Mary would always find something to complain about, whether it was the food, the temperature, or the way Linda had arranged her belongings. Linda tried her best to be patient, but sometimes it became overwhelming.

"GUILT CAN HAVE A SIGNIFICANT IMPACT ON CAREGIVERS."

One day, after a particularly difficult morning, Linda found herself sitting on the porch, tears rolling down her cheeks. She felt guilty for feeling frustrated with Mary. After all, Mary had been there for her when she was growing up. Linda knew that Mary couldn't help being the way she was, but she couldn't help feeling overwhelmed and exhausted.

Linda's daughter came out to check on her and saw her crying. She hugged her mom and sat down next to her on the porch. Linda told her daughter how guilty she felt for being frustrated with Mary, and how she didn't know how much longer she could keep up with the demands of being a caregiver.

Her daughter listened patiently and told her that it was okay to feel frustrated. It didn't mean that Linda loved Mary any less. Caregiving was a difficult and demanding job, and it was natural to feel overwhelmed at times. She also reminded Linda that taking care of herself was just as important as taking care of Mary.

Linda realized that her daughter was right. She needed to take care of herself and find ways to cope with the stress of caregiving. She started taking breaks throughout the day to do things she enjoyed, like reading or gardening. She also started going to a support group for caregivers, where she found comfort in talking to others who were going through the same thing.

Over time, Linda learned to manage her frustration and guilt. She realized that it was possible to love someone and still feel frustrated with them. Most importantly, she learned that taking care of herself was essential to being a good caregiver.

Guilt can have a significant impact on caregivers as they often experience guilt related to their role. It can also arise from difficult decisions, such as deciding to place a loved one in a care facility or making end-of-life decisions.

The emotional toll of caregiving is substantial, and guilt can contribute to feelings of stress, anxiety, and depression. Caregivers may feel as though are failing their loved one, which can lead to feelings of helplessness and frustration.

Caregivers may also experience physical effects of guilt, such as fatigue, headaches, and other stress-related symptoms. Guilt can also impact relationships with friends and family members, as caregivers may withdraw from social activities or feel like they are burdening others with their responsibilities.

It is important for caregivers to address feelings of guilt and seek support when needed. This may include talking with a trusted friend or family member, joining a support group, or seeking professional counseling. Caregivers should also prioritize self-care and take time for themselves to prevent burnout and manage stress.

"IT IS IMPORTANT FOR SIBLINGS TO ACKNOWLEDGE AND ADDRESS THEIR FEELINGS OF GUILT."

Here are some tips that may help you handle guilt associated with caregiving:

Recognize that it's normal to feel guilty: It's important to understand that feeling guilty is a normal and common experience for caregivers. You're not alone in feeling this way.

Identify the source of your guilt: Try to figure out what is causing you to feel guilty. Is it because you feel like you're not doing enough? Or because you feel like you're neglecting other responsibilities? Understanding the source of your guilt can help you address it.

Talk to someone: Sharing your feelings with a trusted friend, family member, or therapist can help you process your emotions and gain a new perspective on your situation.

Practice self-compassion: Be kind to yourself and acknowledge that you're doing the best you can in a challenging situation. Treat yourself the way you would treat a friend in need. Be kind, understanding, and patient with yourself. Remind yourself that you're doing something important and valuable by caring for your loved one.

Take care of yourself: It's important to take care of your own needs and well-being, too. Make time for yourself, engage in self-care activities, and seek support when you need it.

Consider seeking professional help: If your guilt is causing significant distress or interfering with your ability to function, it may be helpful to speak with a mental health professional who can help you work through your feelings and develop coping strategies.

Overcoming caregiver guilt is about recognizing your limitations, being kind to yourself, and breaking the cycle of self-blame. Remember that you are doing enough, and your love and care are invaluable. Prioritize self-care and seek help if you need it. By taking care of yourself and seeking support when you need it, you can better manage your feelings and provide the best possible care for your loved one. Caregiving can be challenging, but with the right mind-set and support, you can overcome any obstacle.

"SOME SIBLINGS MAY FEEL RESENTFUL TOWARDS THEIR SIBLINGS WHO ARE MORE INVOLVED."

Siblings and Guilt

It is common for siblings who do not play an active role in caring for their ailing aging parents to experience feelings of guilt. They may feel guilty for not doing enough to help their parents or for not being there for them when they needed it.

There are several ways in which siblings who don't care for ailing aging parents may express their guilt:

Apologizing: Siblings may apologize to their parents for not being there for them as much as they should have been.

Avoidance: Some siblings may avoid spending time with their parents or discussing their care, as they feel guilty about not being more involved.

Defensive behavior: Siblings who feel guilty may become defensive when their level of involvement in their parents' care is questioned.

Overcompensation: Other siblings may overcompensate by trying to make up for their lack of involvement by doing more than their fair share of caregiving tasks.

Resentment: Some siblings may feel resentful towards their siblings who are more involved in their parents' care, as they feel guilty about not doing more themselves.

Where is Frank Jr.?

Frank Jr. had always been distant from his father, Frank Sr. He had his own life and priorities, and taking care of his aging father was not one of them. Meanwhile, Frank Sr.'s health was deteriorating with each passing day, and his daughter Frances could see it all too clearly. She had given up her own career and moved her father into her home to care for him.

As the months passed, Frank Jr. became consumed with his work and personal life, neglecting to check in on his father or assist his sister in any way. Although he was aware of his sister's situation, he remained apathetic towards it.

However, Frank Sr.'s condition deteriorated to the point where he required hospitalization. Frances faithfully stayed by his side every day, but Frank Jr. was nowhere to be found.

Frank Jr. was overwhelmed with guilt. He recognized that he should have been there for his father and sister, but now it was too late. He couldn't bring himself to visit his father in the hospital, fully aware that he had let him down. He vowed to himself that he would do better once his father was discharged.

But Frank Sr.'s condition continued to deteriorate, and he eventually passed away. Frank Jr. was consumed by guilt and regret. He had missed his chance to make things right with his father and to support his sister in her time of need. He was overwhelmed by the weight of his guilt and didn't know what to do.

He confided in a close friend, who listened patiently and offered some advice. "You can't change the past, but you can change the future," the friend said. "You can't bring your father back, but you can honor his memory by being there for your family now. Reach out to your sister and see if there's anything you can do to help her. It won't undo what's been done, but it's a start."

Frank Jr. took the advice to heart and reached out to his sister. She was still grieving but appreciated the gesture. They talked for hours, and Frank Jr. listened as she recounted her experiences caring for their father. He realized how much she had sacrificed and how little he had done to support her.

"I'm sorry," he said, tears welling up in his eyes. "I should have been there for you and Dad."

Frances took his hand and squeezed it gently. "I know," she said. "But it's okay now. We can move forward from here."

Frank Jr. knew that he had a long way to go to make up for his past mistakes, but he was determined to try. He started visiting his sister more often, helping her with chores, and spending time with her. He even started volunteering at a local senior center, hoping to make a difference in the lives of other seniors in need.

Over time, Frank Jr.'s guilt started to fade, replaced by a sense of purpose and fulfillment. He knew that he could never change the past, but he could make a difference in the present and the future. And he was determined to do just that.

In the end, Frank Jr. realized that the best way to honor his father's memory was to be there for his family and make a positive impact in the world. His journey had been difficult, but he had learned a valuable lesson: it's never too late to do the right thing.

It is important for siblings to acknowledge and address their feelings of guilt in order to move forward and provide supportive for their aging parents. This may involve engaging in open and honest conversations with both their parents and siblings about their emotions and finding opportunities to become more involved in their parents' care if feasible. Additionally, seeking the assistance of a therapist or counselor can be advantageous in working through feelings of guilt and developing strategies to manage caregiving responsibilities.

Frequently Asked Questions: (FAQ's)

What causes guilt in full-time caregivers?

Full-time caregivers may feel guilty for a variety of reasons, including a sense of inadequacy, the desire for personal time and space, and negative emotions towards the person they are caring for.

What are the effects of guilt on full-time caregivers?

Guilt can lead to physical exhaustion, mental fatigue, and emotional distress. Caregivers may experience symptoms such as headaches, body aches, and trouble sleeping.

How can full-time caregivers overcome guilt?

Caregivers can overcome guilt by re framing their perspective, seeking support, practicing self-care, and acknowledging and accepting their feelings of guilt.

What are the results of overcoming guilt for full-time caregivers?

Overcoming guilt can lead to an increase in energy, a more positive outlook, and an improved ability to handle stress. Caregivers may also feel more motivated, experience better sleep, and reengage in activities they once enjoyed.

How can full-time caregivers handle guilt effectively?

Caregivers should prioritize self-care, seek support from family and friends, participate in support groups, or consider therapy to handle guilt effectively.

HELPLESSNESS

Helplessness in full-time caregivers refers to a feeling of powerlessness or lack of control over a situation where they are responsible for the care of another person. Full-time caregivers often provide care for individuals who are unable to care for themselves due to age, illness, or disability. Caregivers may feel overwhelmed and unable to cope with the challenges they face. This can lead to a sense of helplessness, where caregivers feel like their efforts are not making a significant difference in the well-being of the person they are caring for.

Feeling of Helplessness in Full Time Caregivers

Taking care of someone with a chronic illness or disability can be an overwhelming and challenging task. Full-time caregivers often struggle with feelings of helplessness, which can lead to physical, emotional, and mental exhaustion. On this topic, we will discuss the causes, effects, signs, and ways of overcoming helplessness in full-time caregivers.

"CAREGIVERS SHOULD NOT BE AFRAID TO ASK FOR HELP"

Causes of Helplessness in Full-time Caregivers

Lack of Support: Many caregivers feel isolated and unsupported. They may not have anyone to discuss their feelings with or may not receive enough help from family, friends, or medical staff.

Inadequate Resources: Caregivers may struggle to access essential resources, such as healthcare, information, and financial assistance.

Physical and Emotional Demands: Caring for someone full-time can be physically and emotionally draining, especially if the caregiver has to perform demanding tasks like lifting, bathing or managing medications.

Effects of Helplessness in Full-time Caregivers

Stress and Anxiety: Caregiving can be a significant source of stress and anxiety, which can lead to a higher risk of depression, chronic illness and a diminished quality of life.

Physical Exhaustion: Caregiving can cause physical exhaustion, leading to feelings of fatigue, headaches, muscle pain, and other health problems.

Emotional Distress: Frequent exposure to suffering, illness and death can cause significant emotional distress in caregivers.

Signs of Helplessness in Full-time Caregivers

Loss of Interest: Caregivers who feel helpless may experience a lack of interest in activities they once enjoyed.

Fatigue and Burnout: Caregivers may feel emotionally and physically exhausted and experience signs of burnout, such as irritability, anger, and feelings of hopelessness.

Poor Physical Health: Frequent exposure to illness may lead to caregivers neglecting their own health, leading to a higher risk of illness.

Overcoming Helplessness in Full-time Caregivers

Seek Support: Caregivers who feel helpless should seek support from others. This can include family, friends, support groups or healthcare professionals.

Prioritize Self-care: Caregivers should prioritize their self-care by establishing a routine that includes time for rest, exercise, healthy eating and relaxation strategies.

Ask for Help: Caregivers should not be afraid to ask for help whenever necessary. Help can come in the form of respite care, home health services, or hired assistance.

> ## "CAREGIVERS SHOULD TRUST THEMSELVES AND THEIR INSTINCTS."

Results Over Time

Over time, many caregivers find that the skills they develop throughout their caregiving journey can be useful in other areas of their lives, such as improved communication and empathy.

It's OK to Ask For Help!

Julie had always been a devoted daughter, but as her parents got older and their health began to decline, she found herself taking on more and more responsibility as their primary caregiver. Living just five miles away, she felt it was her duty to ensure that her parents were well taken care of, but the burden was starting to take its toll.

With a full-time job and a family of her own to care for, Julie struggled to balance it all. She spent most of her evenings and weekends running errands, handling doctor's appointments, managing medications, and making sure her parents had everything they needed. It was a never-ending cycle of exhaustion and stress.

Despite her best efforts, Julie found herself feeling overwhelmed and helpless. No matter how much she did, it never seemed to be enough. She was constantly worried about missing something important or making a mistake that could have serious consequences.

One day, after missing one of her dad's appointments, Julie hit rock bottom. She felt like a failure and couldn't shake the feeling of helplessness that had taken hold. She knew she needed to do something to regain her perspective and find a way to manage her caregiver responsibilities without sacrificing her own well-being.

She reached out to a local caregiver support group and found comfort in talking to others who were going through similar experiences. She also talked to her employer about the possibility of working from home a few days a week to better manage her schedule. With their support, she was able to take a step back and focus on her own needs while still being there for her parents.

Julie learned that it was okay to ask for help and that she didn't have to do everything on her own. She started delegating some tasks to other family members and hired a part-time caregiver to help with the day-to-day responsibilities. With this support system in place, Julie was able to regain her perspective and find a sense of balance in her life.

While caring for her parents was still tough, Julie no longer felt helpless. She was able to focus on what was truly important – spending quality time with her parents and cherishing the moments they had together.

How to Handle Helplessness in Caregivers

Practice Mindfulness: Caregivers can practice mindfulness to be more present and focused, decreasing feelings of overwhelm and increasing their ability to cope effectively.

Trust Yourself

Caregivers should trust themselves and their instincts. The role of caregiver requires making difficult decisions, and following intuition can be the best course of action.

Take Breaks Regularly

Caregivers should take regular breaks to recharge, and the person they care for can receive the best care when the caregiver is also at optimal health.

In conclusion, caring for someone full-time can be challenging, overwhelming, and emotionally draining. Caregivers can experience feelings of helplessness, which can worsen without proper support, care, and treatment. It is crucial for caregivers to seek support, prioritize self-care, and ask for help whenever necessary. Techniques such as mindfulness, trusting oneself, and taking regular breaks can go a long way in combating feelings of helplessness and burnout.

Frequently Asked Questions: (FAQs)

How do I know if I am experiencing caregiver burnout?

Some signs of caregiver burnout include physical and mental exhaustion, feeling overwhelmed, and loss of interest in activities.

How can I prioritize self-care when I am always busy with caregiving duties?

It's crucial to schedule time for self-care and ask for help from family and friends or hire a professional caregiver to free up time.

Is there any financial assistance available for full-time caregivers?

Yes, some programs offer financial assistance for caregivers. Check with your community resources or healthcare providers for more details.

Can support groups really make a difference in managing caregiver stress?

Yes, support groups offer emotional support, practical advice, and a sense of community that can help manage caregiver stress more effectively.

How does mindfulness help caregivers manage their stress?

Mindfulness practices, such as meditation, help reduce stress by promoting relaxation and present-moment awareness. It can increase resilience and boost the overall well-being of caregivers.

Is it normal to feel guilty or ashamed for needing help as a full-time caregiver?

No, it is not unusual to feel guilty or ashamed at times as a caregiver. However, it is crucial to acknowledge these feelings and seek help whenever necessary.

HOPELESSNESS

Hopelessness is the feeling that nothing can be done to improve a situation. It is a common feeling among full-time caregivers who are caring for their loved ones, but the demands of caregiving are too overwhelming. The word 'hopeless' can be attributed to caregivers as they often have few breaks and little time for self-care. Full-time caregiving can quickly become a 24/7 job, leaving little hope for relief. Without proper support caregivers can find themselves struggling to see the light at the end of the tunnel.

Hopelessness can lead to despair, depression, and burnout and may affect the quality of care they provide. Knowing the signs of hopelessness is crucial in getting the right care and support.

Being a full-time caregiver can be an overwhelming job. The person in this position is responsible for a multitude of tasks including administering medication, coordinating doctor's appointments, handling finances, assisting with bathing and grooming, and ensuring their loved one is safe and well-cared for. All of these duties are challenging and can lead to feelings of hopelessness in caregivers.

"HOPELESSNESS CAN INDUCE FEELINGS OF
WORTHLESSNESS."

One of the most common issues that full-time caregivers face is hopelessness, which can manifest itself in many ways. In this article, we will explore the difference between burnout and hopelessness in caregivers, discuss how support groups can help alleviate feelings of hopelessness, and examine the relationship between hopelessness and stress.

What is the difference between burnout and hopelessness in caregivers?

Caregiver burnout is a state of physical, emotional, and mental exhaustion that can occur when a person is responsible for the continuous care of a loved one. This condition can lead to fatigue, sleep deprivation, and a sense of detachment from the outside world. Burnout can be severe but is generally temporary and can be treated through a combination of rest, support, and self-care.

On the other hand, caregiver hopelessness is an overwhelming feeling of despair or a loss of self-efficacy. Unlike burnout, hopelessness can extend beyond caregiving responsibilities and can harm a caregiver's general quality of life. Hopelessness can induce feelings of worthlessness and enhance existing mental health disorders like depression and anxiety.

How can caregiving support groups help with feelings of hopelessness?

Caregiving support groups are an effective way to work with fellow caregivers and healthcare professionals to provide essential care for their loved ones. In these groups, caregivers can share their experiences, ask questions, and learn from other caregivers. Members can also receive emotional, educational, and social support and be a foundation of hope for one another.

Notably, caregivers often feel lonely or isolated, which adds to their mental load. Support groups are an excellent place to find understanding individuals who are facing similar challenges. Therefore, joining a support group can be a powerful tool in combating caregiver hopelessness.

Can hopelessness lead to caregiving-related stress?

Yes, hopelessness is directly related to caregiving-related stress. As discussed earlier, caregiver hopelessness can significantly affect a caregiver's emotional well-being, leading to increased stress and anxiety. Hopelessness can make it harder to manage decision-making, amplifying feelings of stress and contributing to physical symptoms like fatigue, digestive problems, sleep disturbances, and headaches. Reevaluating daily caregiving routines, seeking support, and practicing self-care activities are essential steps towards managing caregiver stress.

"HOPELESSNESS CAN LEAD TO DESPAIR, DEPRESSION, AND BURNOUT."

It's Hopeless...

Angel's heart sank as she received the news from her mom's doctor. Her mom, Maria, had been diagnosed with a chronic illness, but the doctors weren't sure what it was. Angel tried to hide her despair, but it was difficult as she had a huge meeting coming up at work. Being an executive in a major center city company in downtown Chicago came with its own stress, but now, with her mom's condition added to the mix, it seemed impossible to manage.

Maria doesn't speak English, and Angel found it hard to juggle her mom's situation with the upcoming meeting, making her feel emotionally drained, despairing, and anxious. These feelings which started to show up physically as headaches, fatigue, and stomach issues.

Angel's work was her passion, but being an only child to her mom, she couldn't ignore the new demands placed on her life. Angel felt the weight of the responsibility, but also the helplessness she faced due to the language barrier. To add to her worries, Maria's condition wasn't improving, and she was missing work. Angel felt as hopeless as her situation.

Angel had regular conversations with her good friend Gabriele, who worked in the same company, and was the only person at her workplace who knew about her mom's condition. Gabriele's empathetic personality made her the perfect person for Angel to confide in. She suggested taking time off work, but Angel felt conflicted and worried if her absence might negatively impact her job. Gabriele understood and offered to be there for her in whatever way Angel needed her. They both left for lunch, and Gabriele helped Angel confront her feelings about not being able to manage both situations at once.

Angel was hesitant to inform her boss, but the situation had reaching a breaking point. She could no longer juggle her mom's illness and her work. Finally, Angel mustered the courage to have a conversation with her boss about her situation. Angel explained the language barrier issue to her boss and how it affected her ability to care for her mom while dealing with a demanding job. Her boss listened, attentively, and Angel felt grateful for their support. In fact, her boss not only empthized with her situation but also expressed admiration for how Angel had been managing her work thus far. For the first time, Angel felt like the weight on her shoulders had been lifted.

"THE EFFECTS OF HOPELESSNESS CAN BE DAMAGING; SEEK HELP BEFORE IT BECOMES TOO OVERWHELMING."

The language barrier came into play when Angel took her mom to the doctor's office. The doctor spoke English, but her mom didn't understand the medical jargon, and it was frustrating for both Angel and Maria. "What does that mean?" was a common question that Maria asked Angel, and Angel would explain what the doctor meant in Spanish. However, Angel still didn't understand fully what was happening with her mom.

"Is there any progress?" Angel would ask, to which the doctor would say, "We are still waiting for further tests; we will keep you informed." These conversations were frustrating because there was no definitive answer which made Angel more and more depressed.

Angel felt that when words fail, emotion speaks louder. The fear of the unknown was the worst feeling, but caring for her mom and keeping up with her job was even more overwhelming. Angel tried to manage both the best she could, but sometimes it seemed that there weren't enough hours in a day. Sometimes, Angel would force a smile to cover up her unease in front of her mom when she felt like breaking down.

Sometimes, all it takes is one act of kindness to improve your day. At work, Angel received a package that was dropped off at her workplace desk. It was a gourmet basket with a note from Gabriele that read, "Thinking of you! Hope this brightens your day!" The gesture made a big difference to Angel, and she felt incredibly grateful for the support she received from her friend, even on such a small scale.

Angel recognized that her mother's medical condition wasn't going to be easy and that it would continue to affect her work life. She needed to find ways to cope with the added stress on both fronts. Angel also realized that sharing her experience with those closest to her made a big difference.

By communicating with her boss, friend, and doctor, Angel was able to manage her work and mom's care a lot more effectively. This wasn't something she could manage on her own, and the support she received made a difference. Angel still had to juggle her time effectively, but knowing that her support system had her back felt empowering.

Being an executive at a major center city company in downtown Chicago came with its own set of demands. Adding Maria's illness to the mix was a significant challenge for Angel, who took on the role of caregiver for her mom. But through communication and support,

Angel was able to balance both situations and move forward in her job and her life.

Angel's experience is one that is recognizable to many and emphasizes that it's ok to ask for help when needed. By confiding in those closest to her, Angel was able to gain the support she needed, allowing her to be the caregiver her mom needed and the executive her job required.

What are the effects of hopelessness?

The effects of hopelessness can be damaging, and it's important to seek help before it becomes too overwhelming. Hopelessness can lead to depression, health problems, and strained relationships with loved ones. Additionally, it can affect the quality of care the caregiver provides, leading to neglect of their loved one's needs.

What can caregivers do to prevent or alleviate hopelessness?

There are various techniques that can be helpful, including exercise, meditation, or talking to a therapist. Caregivers should also seek out support systems where they can connect with other caregivers, as this can be an excellent way to manage stress and gain helpful advice.

Staying positive is another important factor in preventing hopelessness. Finding joy in the small moments can make a huge difference in a caregiver's outlook. Caregivers can also seek out activities that bring them pleasure and provide an escape from caregiving responsibilities.

Finally, understanding the needs of caregivers is crucial. Caregivers need support and understanding from their loved ones, and it's important to recognize that caregiving is a job that requires immense amounts of patience and dedication. By recognizing these needs and providing support, caregivers can feel motivated to continue providing care in the best way possible.

"HOPELESSNESS IS A COMMON FEELING AMONG FULL-TIME CAREGIVERS."

As a caregiver, experiencing hopelessness can be overwhelming. Symptoms like stress, anxiety, and depression can impact one's quality of life and overall health. While hopelessness is common among caregivers, it is essential to recognize the signs and practice self-care, join a support group or seek professional help to overcome it. As discussed throughout this topic, there are various ways to address hopelessness, including support groups, and therapeutic exercises. Therefore, caregivers must feel empowered to prioritize their mental and emotional well-being concerning their caregiving responsibilities.

In conclusion, hopelessness is a common feeling among full-time caregivers, and it's important to address this issue by seeking out support, finding appropriate coping mechanisms, and staying positive. Caregivers need to recognize that they are not alone in their struggles and should not be afraid to ask for help when needed.

Frequently Asked Questions: (FAQs)

What can caregivers do to prevent hopelessness?

Caregivers can take steps such as seeking support systems, taking breaks, and engaging in activities that bring them joy to prevent hopelessness.

What is the difference between burnout and hopelessness in caregivers?

Burnout is a state of physical, emotional, and mental exhaustion that can occur when a person is responsible for the continuous care of a loved one. In contrast, caregiver hopelessness is an overwhelming feeling of despair or loss of self-efficacy. It can extend beyond the specific caregiving responsibilities and harm a caregiver's overall quality of life.

How can caregiving support groups help with feelings of hopelessness?

Caregiving support groups are an effective way to work with fellow caregivers and healthcare professionals to provide crucial care for their loved ones. Joining a support group can help combat caregiver hopelessness by offering emotional, educational, and social support.

Can hopelessness lead to caregiving-related stress?

Yes, caregiver hopelessness directly correlates with caregiver-related stress, leading to increased stress and anxiety. Hopelessness can make it harder to manage caregiving duties, amplify stress, and contribute to physical symptoms like fatigue, digestive problems, sleep disturbances, and headaches.

How can hopelessness affect the caregiver's loved ones?

Hopelessness can lead to strained relationships with loved ones and neglect of their needs. It's important to address hopelessness to prevent further negative impacts on the caregiver's loved ones.

"Caregiving is Rewarding."

LONELINESS

Loneliness is a subjective feeling of sadness, emptiness, and isolation resulting from a lack of satisfying social connections or meaningful relationships with others. It can be experienced even when one is surrounded by others or in a crowded place. Loneliness is often accompanied by a sense of disconnection or alienation from others and a feeling of being misunderstood or unappreciated. It can have negative effects on a person's mental and physical health, and can lead to depression, anxiety, and other psychological and emotional problems.

Caregiving is a challenging job, whether you're taking care of an aging parent, disabled child, or a sick spouse. It can be rewarding to help improve someone's life, but it can also be draining and isolating. Full-time caregivers, in particular, face a unique set of challenges, including financial strain, constant worry, and a lack of social interaction. These challenges can lead to feelings of loneliness and depression.

Causes of Loneliness in Full-Time Caregivers

Loneliness is the result of a lack of social interaction and feelings of disconnection. Full-time caregivers are more susceptible to feelings of loneliness due to their limited mobility and social isolation. Some of the causes of loneliness in caregivers include:

Financial Strain: Full-time caregiving can cause financial stress, as it often results in lost wages or decreased employment opportunities. The financial strain can affect a caregiver's mental health, leading to feelings of loneliness and isolation.

Lack of Social Interaction: Caregivers often have limited opportunities for social interaction, as they spend most of their time caring for their loved ones. Their social life may revolve around their caregiving responsibilities, causing them to feel isolated and disconnected from their peers.

Burnout: Caregivers who experience burnout may feel emotionally and physically exhausted, leading to a lack of motivation to engage in social activities outside of their caregiving responsibilities. This can result in feelings of loneliness and isolation.

Effects of Loneliness in Caregivers

Loneliness can have serious negative effects on a caregiver's mental and physical health, including:

Depression: Caregivers who experience loneliness are more likely to develop depression. The lack of social interaction and feelings of isolation can result in sadness, hopelessness, and a lack of motivation.

Reduced Quality of Life: Loneliness can affect a caregiver's overall quality of life. The lack of social interaction and feelings of disconnection can lead to decreased enjoyment in activities, a diminished sense of purpose, and a lack of fulfillment.

Physical Health Issues: Loneliness can also negatively affect a caregiver's physical health. The stress and emotional toll of caregiving can lead to chronic health problems, such as high blood pressure, heart disease, and a weakened immune system.

More Alone Than Ever

Judith had always been the life of the party. With her infectious smile and bubbly personality, she had no shortage of friends. She was always the first to organize a night out, and her phone buzzed constantly with messages from her friends asking her to join them for drinks or a movie.

But all that changed when her mother was diagnosed with dementia.

Judith had always been close to her mother, and she knew that caring for her would be a full-time job. She quit her job and moved in with her mother, determined to give her the best care possible. However, as the months turned into years, Judith found herself becoming increasingly isolated.

Her friends still reached out to her at first, but as time went on, they stopped calling. They didn't understand the toll that caring for someone with dementia was taking on her. Judith was exhausted all the time, barely getting any sleep at night as she tended to her mother's needs.

The once-bustling house was now quiet, except for the sound of her mother's occasional outbursts. Judith's phone rarely rang, and when it did, it was usually a telemarketer. She felt like she was living in a completely different world than her friends, who were still going out and having fun.

Judith tried to keep in touch with her friends, but she found that she had less and less to talk about. Her days were consumed with caring for her mother, and she had little energy left for anything else. She felt like she was losing touch with the world, and that the world was losing touch with her.

As the years went by, Judith's mother's condition deteriorated. She became increasingly aggressive and violent, making it even harder for Judith to care for her. Judith's health began to suffer as well, both physically and mentally. She was constantly exhausted and on edge, and she found it hard to cope with the overwhelming sense of loneliness that surrounded her.

"CAREGIVERS WHO EXPERIENCE LONELINESS ARE MORE LIKELY TO DEVELOP DEPRESSION."

One day, Judith's mother passed away. Judith was devastated, but she also felt a sense of relief. She had been caring for her mother for so long that it was hard to imagine life without her. But she knew that she needed to start rebuilding her life.

She reached out to her old friends, hoping to reconnect with them. But she found that they had all moved on with their lives. They were married now, with children and jobs and responsibilities. They didn't have time for Judith and her problems.

Judith felt more alone than ever before. She had lost her mother, her friends, and her sense of purpose. She didn't know how to move forward, or if she even wanted to. All she knew was that she didn't want to feel this lonely anymore.

Signs of Loneliness in Caregivers

Identifying the signs of loneliness in caregivers can be crucial in preventing its negative effects. Some of the signs of loneliness in caregivers include:

Fatigue: Feeling tired or exhausted despite getting enough sleep can be a sign of loneliness. Caregivers who feel lonely may have no energy or motivation to engage in activities outside of their caregiving responsibilities.

Social Isolation: If a caregiver is not participating in social activities or spends most of their time alone, they may be experiencing social isolation.

Feelings of Sadness or Depression: Caregivers who are feeling lonely may experience feelings of sadness or depression. They may feel hopeless, unmotivated, and struggle to find joy in activities they once enjoyed.

Overcoming Loneliness in Caregivers: Overcoming loneliness in caregivers can take time and effort, but it is possible. Here are some ways caregivers can overcome loneliness:

Seek Social Support: Joining a support group, engaging in online communities, or attending social events can provide an opportunity for caregivers to connect with others who understand their experiences.

"MANAGING LONELINESS IS AN ONGOING PROCESS FOR CAREGIVERS."

No Longer Lonely

Anita always knew that being a full-time caregiver for her mother, Deana, would be a challenging task. Deana, a single mother became completely deaf shortly after Anita was born. Since then she relied solely on Anita for her daily needs. Living in a rural area of Edenton, North Carolina, with few visitors or relatives, Anita's only daily company was her mother.

As time passed, Anita found herself becoming increasingly lonely. She rarely left the house, and when she did, it was only to run errands or take her mother to the doctor. She She yearned for a relationship, but the harsh reality of their situation meant that it was nearly impossible.

Winter arrived, bringing with it the snow. Cabin fever set in, and Anita found herself talking to herself out loud. She knew it wasn't healthy, but she couldn't help it. She needed someone to talk to, someone to listen to her.

Desperate for a connection to humanity, Anita turned to the internet. She spent hours scrolling through social media, reading blogs, and watching videos, but it wasn't enough. She craved a more personal connection.

One day, she stumbled upon an online forum for caregivers. At first, she was hesitant, but she decided to give it a try. She introduced herself and shared her story. To her surprise, she received an outpouring of support from complete strangers. They shared their own experiences, offered advice, and even just listened.

Over the next few months, Anita spent more and more time on the forum. She made friends, and they talked about everything from their daily struggles to their hopes and dreams. It became a lifeline for Anita, and she felt like a weight had been lifted off her shoulders.

Through it all, Anita never neglected her responsibilities as a caregiver. She continued to care for her mother with love and dedication. But now, she had a community to turn to when she needed support.

As the snow melted and spring arrived, Anita realized that she had overcome her loneliness. She had found a way to connect with humanity, even if it was only virtually. She was no longer talking to herself out loud, but to a group of people who understood her struggles and were there for her.

Anita knew that caring for her mother would still be a challenging task, but she was no longer alone. She had found a community of caregivers who had become her friends and her support system. And with that, she knew that she could face any challenge that came her way.

Take Care of Yourself

Practicing self-care can reduce stress and improve overall well-being. Caregivers should prioritize their physical and emotional health by eating well, exercising regularly, and finding time for activities they enjoy.

Reach Out for Help

Caregivers can ask for help from friends, family, or community resources to reduce their caregiving responsibilities and create more time for social interaction.

Results Over Time

Managing loneliness is an ongoing process for caregivers. The strategies mentioned can help alleviate loneliness in the short-term, but caregivers must continue to seek social support and prioritize self-care to maintain mental and physical well-being in the long term.

"LONELINESS IS A COMMON EXPERIENCE AMONG CAREGIVERS, ESPECIALLY THOSE WHO PROVIDE FULL-TIME CARE."

How to Handle Loneliness as a Caregiver

Handling loneliness as a caregiver can be challenging, but there are ways to manage it. Here are some tips for caregivers:

Recognize that Loneliness is Normal: Loneliness is a common experience for caregivers. Recognizing that it's normal to feel lonely can help caregivers take steps to manage these feelings.

Prioritize Self-Care: Taking care of oneself should be a top priority for caregivers. Self-care can include physical exercise, engaging in hobbies, or seeking professional support.

Take Advantage of Technology; Smart phones, computers, and other devices can provide a way for caregivers to connect with others virtually. Social media, video chats, and online gaming can help caregivers stay connected to their friends and family.

Finally, loneliness can be a difficult feeling to manage, and it's especially challenging for full-time caregivers. However, by recognizing the signs and causes of loneliness and taking practical steps to manage it, caregivers can prioritize their emotional and physical well-being. Remember to seek social support, practice self-care, and take advantage of technology to stay connected to friends and family.

Frequently Asked Questions: (FAQ's)

Is it normal for caregivers to feel lonely?

Yes, loneliness is a common experience among caregivers, especially those who provide full-time care.

What are some ways to prevent loneliness in full-time caregivers?

Seeking social support, making time for self-care and leisure activities, and practicing stress-reducing techniques can help prevent loneliness in full-time caregivers.

Can loneliness in full-time caregivers lead to depression?

Yes, loneliness can increase the risk of depression and other mental health issues in full-time caregivers.

What resources are available to help caregivers overcome loneliness?

Support groups, respite care, and professional counseling or therapy are all resources that can help caregivers overcome loneliness.

How can I find a caregiver support group?

You can search for caregiver support groups in your area through websites like AARP.

---

*"Caregivers
Need
Balance."*

REGRET

Regret, as a full-time caregiver can encompass feelings of disappointment, sadness, or guilt that arise from a perceived or real failure to adequately care for a loved one. Caregivers may experience regret for various reasons, such as not being able to provide sufficient attention or support, believing they made the incorrect decisions regarding medical treatments or care arrangements, or feeling that they have sacrificed their own well-being and personal goals to fulfill their caregiving responsibilities. Regret is a normal and understandable part of the caregiving journey, but it can also indicate burnout or emotional distress. It is crucial for caregivers to seek support and resources to help them cope with their feelings of regret and maintain their own well-being.

Caring for a loved one can be both rewarding and fulfilling, but it can also be incredibly exhausting and stressful. Full-time caregivers face a unique set of challenges, from managing daily responsibilities to dealing with the emotional toll it takes on them. One common struggle that caregivers experience is regret. In this article, we will discuss the causes, effects, signs, and ways of overcoming the regretful feelings that full-time caregivers may have.

"REGRET CAN LEAD TO FEELINGS OF HOPELESSNESS AND HELPLESSNESS."

Causes of Regret

Taking care of a family member can have a negative impact on both your mental and physical health, which can lead to feelings of regret. Here are some common reasons why caregivers may experience regret:

Lack of Support: When caregivers do not receive support from their family and friends, it can make the caregiving journey even more challenging. This lack of support can result in feelings of loneliness and isolation, causing caregivers to regret not having someone to turn to for emotional support.

Missed Opportunities: Providing 24/7 care leaves little time for other activities, such as work, hobbies, and social outings. Caregivers may regret missing out on these opportunities and feel like they have lost a part of their own life.

Financial Strain: Providing full-time care can be expensive, leading to financial difficulties. Caregivers may regret not being able to provide better care due to financial constraints.

I Wish I Never Volunteered

Anthony had always been a family man, so when his Uncle Angelo fell ill and needed a full-time caregiver, he didn't hesitate to volunteer. His brother Paul and sister Maria, who lived nearby, also offered to help. At first, everything went smoothly, and the siblings took turns caring for their uncle.

However, as time went by, Paulie and Maria became more and more involved in their own family affairs, leaving Anthony to shoulder the bulk of the caregiving responsibilities. Anthony found himself spending long hours taking care of his uncle, which left him little time for his own family or friends.

One day, Anthony's frustration boiled over, and he confronted his siblings about their lack of support. "I can't do this alone anymore," he said. "I need your help. You can't just leave me to take care of Uncle Ange by myself."

Paulie and Maria were taken aback by Anthony's outburst. "We have our own families to take care of," Paulie said. "We can't just drop everything to take care of Uncle Angelo."

Maria chimed in, "And what about all the times you couldn't help us because you were taking care of him? We've all had to make sacrifices."

But Anthony was not appeased. "I understand that, but I feel like I'm the only one who's been taking care of Uncle Ange lately. It's not fair."

The argument continued for some time, with neither side willing to compromise. In the end, Anthony felt overwhelmed and bitter. "I wish I never volunteered for this," he said regretfully.

Eventually, things reached a breaking point when Anthony fell ill due to the stress of taking care of their uncle. This was a wake-up call for Paulie and Maria, who finally understood the immense sacrifices Anthony had been making. They decided to step up and take on more caregiving responsibilities, giving Anthony the opportunity to rest and recuperate.

As time passed, the siblings grew closer as they went through this experience together. They learned how to communicate more effectively and provide support for one another. Although taking care of their uncle remained a difficult task, they faced it as a united family.

Effects of Regret

Regret can take a significant toll on the physical and emotional well-being of caregivers.

Here are some common effects of regretful feelings:
Depression and Anxiety: Regret can lead to feelings of hopelessness and helplessness, resulting in depression and anxiety.

Loss of Joy: Caregivers may lose the joy they once found in the care they provide, leading to feelings of dissatisfaction and resentment.

Burnout: Regretful feelings can contribute to caregiver burnout and make it difficult to continue providing care.

Signs of Regret in Caregivers

It is essential to recognize the signs of regret in caregivers to address the issue effectively. Here are some common signs:

Withdrawal: Caregivers may withdraw from social engagements and activities they once enjoyed.

Irritability: Caregivers may display signs of irritability, anger, and frustration.

Emotional Distress: Caregivers may experience emotional distress, such as depression and anxiety.

Overcoming Regret

Overcoming feelings of regret in full-time caregivers can be challenging, but it is possible. Here are some ways to overcome regret:

Seek Support: Caregivers should seek emotional support from family and friends, a therapist, or a support group.

Focus on the Present: Caregivers can reduce feelings of regret by focusing on the present and accepting the situation as it is.

Practice Self-Care: Caregivers should prioritize self-care and practice activities that promote physical and emotional well-being, such as exercise, meditation, and hobbies.

How to Handle Regret

Handling regret requires self-reflection and seeking support. Caregivers should acknowledge their regrets and take steps to address them. Seeking support from a therapist or support group can provide additional guidance and coping strategies.

Regret is a common struggle among full-time caregivers, but with the right coping strategies, it is possible to overcome these feelings. Seeking support, focusing on the present, and practicing self-care can contribute to long-term improvement in caregiver well-being. It is essential to recognize the signs of regret and take steps to address these feelings, such as speaking with a therapist or joining a support group. Caring for a loved one is a challenging task, and it is essential to prioritize self-care and seek support in the process.

Frequently Asked Questions: (FAQs)

What are some common causes of regretful feelings in full-time caregivers?

Common causes include loss of personal freedom and identity, financial strain, and the emotional toll of caring for someone with a chronic illness or disability.

Can regretful feelings in caregivers lead to substance abuse?

Yes, regretful feelings may contribute to substance abuse. Caregivers experiencing stress and regret may turn to drugs or alcohol as a coping mechanism.

Can therapy help caregivers overcome regret?

Yes, therapy can help caregivers overcome feelings of regret. A therapist can offer guidance, coping strategies, and emotional support. Therapy can also provide a safe space for caregivers to process and address their regrets.

Can caregivers have feelings of regret even when they choose to provide care?

Yes, caregivers may still experience feelings of regret, even when they choose to provide care. It is common to feel overwhelmed and regretful in challenging situations.

Can an increase in social support decrease feelings of regret in caregivers?

Yes, increased social support can decrease feelings of regret in caregivers. Caregivers who have a strong support network may experience fewer feelings of isolation and loneliness.

Can regretful feelings in caregivers lead to abuse of their loved ones?

Regretful feelings may contribute to neglect or abuse in rare cases. However, seeking support and addressing feelings of regret can prevent neglect or abuse from occurring.

Can therapy help caregivers overcome regret?

Yes, therapy can help caregivers overcome feelings of regret. A therapist can offer guidance, coping strategies, and emotional support. Therapy can also provide a safe space for caregivers to process and address their regrets.

STRESS

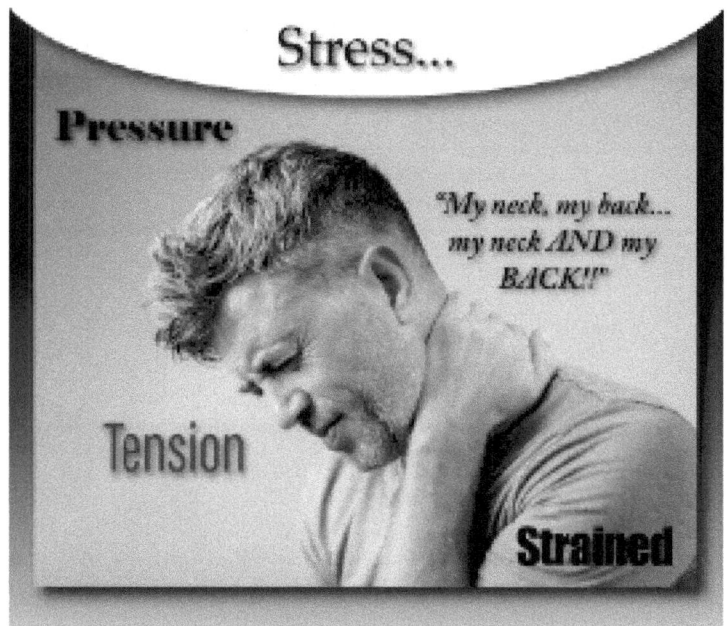

Stress is the body's natural response to a perceived threat or demand. It can manifest in various ways, including physical, emotional, and behavioral symptoms, and can be caused by both positive and negative events. Stress is a part of life and can be beneficial in small doses, but chronic stress can have detrimental effects on physical and mental health.

For full-time caregivers, stress is a common experience. The demands and responsibilities that come with caring for a loved one can leave caregivers feeling overwhelmed, anxious, and emotionally drained.

As a caregiver, taking care of a loved one can bring joy and fulfillment into your life, but it can also bring a lot of stress. Caregiver stress is prevalent, but it is often overlooked and poorly understood. Long-term stress can lead to serious health problems for the caregiver such as depression, anxiety, high blood pressure, and heart disease. Caregivers must balance the needs of their loved ones with their own needs and responsibilities. This balancing act can be difficult and can cause significant stress. In this section we will explore the causes, effects, signs, and solutions to caregiver stress.

"MANAGING STRESS CAN IMPROVE RELATIONSHIPS WITH FAMILY AND FRIENDS."

Causes of Caregiver Stress

Caregivers can experience stress for a number of reasons, including lack of support, isolation, financial strain, and dealing with complex medical issues. Providing care for a loved one can be isolating, and caregivers often feel alone and unsupported. Financial stress is another common cause of caregiver stress. When a caregiver is unable to work full-time and must rely on savings or support from other family members, it can cause significant stress. Another cause of caregiver stress is dealing with complex medical issues. Caregivers must manage medications, appointments, and complicated medical procedures, which can be overwhelming and stressful.

Effects of Caregiver Stress

Long-term stress can lead to serious health problems for the caregiver such as depression, anxiety, high blood pressure, and heart disease. However, the effects of caregiver stress are not limited to physical health. It can also lead to emotional exhaustion and burnout. Caregivers often feel guilty when they

132

take time for themselves, which can lead to resentfulness and anger. Caregivers may also become withdrawn and disconnected from friends and family members, leading to social isolation and loneliness.

A Stressful Story with A Sad Ending

It has been a year since Teisha took on the role of being her mother's full-time caregiver. Teisha had no idea how much it would affect her mental, emotional, and physical well-being. What started as a simple act of love and care became a severe source of stress that haunts her every day.

Teisha's mother Louise had always been her closest confidante and ally. She was the strong one who supported Teisha through her mind-boggling projects in college. As the years passed, Louise developed some health issues that she didn't quite attend to well enough. One day, she had a massive heart attack that left her dependent on others for her daily tasks. Teisha wanted to repay the debt of kindness and care that her mother had given her all these years, so she became her mother's full-time caregiver.

Teisha felt the weight of the world on her shoulders as she stepped into her mother's room, noticing the tired lines etched on her face. Louise, her mother, sat in a chair, clutching a photograph album with her frail hands. Teisha took a deep breath and mustered a smile.

"Good morning, Mom. How are you feeling today?" she asked, hoping to keep the conversation light.

Louise looked up; her eyes distant yet searching. "I don't know, Teisha. I'm scared. I feel like I'm losing myself."

Teisha's heart sank. She sat down next to her mother and held her hand. "You're not alone, Mom. I'm here for you, always."

Louise nodded, tears welling in her eyes. "I know, Teisha. But I see how tired you are. You're trying to do it all, and it's breaking my heart."

A sigh escaped Teisha's lips, her voice tinged with exhaustion. "I thought I had a support system, Mom, but they've backed out one by one. Where are these so called friends when you need them most?"

Louise's voice trembled with sadness. "I never wanted this burden for you, my dear. I never wanted to be a source of stress and hardship."

Tears streamed down Teisha's face, her voice choked with emotion. "You're not, Mom. It's not your fault. I just wish things were different."

They sat in silence for a moment, their shared pain hanging heavy in the room. Then, Louise spoke softly, her words filled with resignation. "Sometimes life doesn't give us the happy ending we hope for, Teisha. We have to find strength in the midst of the storms."

Teisha wiped away her tears, her voice quivering. "I'm trying, Mom. But it's so hard. I feel like I'm drowning."

Louise reached out and held her daughter's face, her touch gentle and filled with love. "You're stronger than you know, my dear. Remember to take care of yourself, too. Your well-being matters."

Teisha nodded, her voice filled with determination. "I won't give up, Mom. I'll keep fighting for us."

As the days turned into weeks and the weeks into months, Teisha's burden grew heavier. The stress continued to mount, taking a toll on her physical and mental health. She tried her best to find moments of respite, but the weight of her responsibilities threatened to crush her.

From running errands to performing personal hygiene tasks, Teisha became the sole caregiver. She even had to quit her full-time job and switch to a part-time one. Despite all her efforts, the caregiving tasks never seem to end, as her mother's condition worsens over with time.

"CAREGIVERS MUST BALANCE THE NEEDS OF THEIR LOVED ONES WITH THEIR OWN NEEDS."

What's more, the social support she was counting on didn't show up when she needed them the most. Friends and family members who initially promised to assist her, backed out, leaving Teisha bitter and exhausted. Teisha feels like she's reached the end of her rope.

Teisha's mom Louise knows how much care Teisha has given her and how much stress that has caused her. Teisha confided in her about feeling overwhelmed and alone. Louise urged her daughter to "never give up," and encouraged her to continue being strong and have faith. However, even as Teisha tried to maintain a positive outlook, it just became too much for her to bear.

Bills pile up as she struggles to make ends meet while caring for her mother. It just seems like there's no happy ending to this story.

Louise, seeing her daughter's anguish, held her hand and whispered, "I'm sorry, Teisha. I'm sorry for the pain I'm causing you."

Teisha's voice was filled with love and desperation. "Don't apologize, Mom. You have nothing to be sorry for. I just wish I could do more for you."

Louise's voice grew weaker, her eyes reflecting deep weariness. "You've done more than enough, my dear. I'm proud of you."

In the end, despite Teisha's unwavering dedication, the story didn't have a happy ending. The weight of caregiving became too much for her to bear, and the financial strain took its toll. Teisha had to make the heartbreaking decision to transition her mother to a nursing home, where professional caregivers could provide the round-the-clock care she needed.

As Teisha visited Louise in the nursing home, tears filled her eyes. "I'm sorry, Mom. I tried my best."

Louise smiled weakly, her voice barely a whisper. "You did, my dear. You did more than anyone could ask for. Remember, life doesn't always give us happy endings. But you showed me love until the very end, and that's what matters."

And with those words, Louise closed her eyes, her journey in this world coming to an end. Teisha's heart shattered, forever marked by the tremendous stress and the bittersweet love she had experienced as a caregiver. She carried the weight of her mother's memory with her, a testament to the sacrifices and challenges faced by caregivers who give their all, even in the absence of a happy ending. Teisha's story is the reality of life as a full-time caregiver. It's also one that's not often talked about, making it difficult for caregivers like Teisha to seek help and support. That's why it's important for all of us to acknowledge the selfless sacrifice that caregivers make in looking after their loved ones. We should extend a helping hand and provide social support whenever we can.

Signs of Caregiver Stress

It can be difficult for caregivers to recognize when they are experiencing stress. Signs of stress can include difficulty sleeping, lack of energy, feelings of hopelessness, and irritability. Caregivers may also experience physical symptoms such as headaches, back pain, and gastrointestinal problems. Additionally, caregivers who are experiencing stress may withdraw from social activities or have difficulty concentrating.

Overcoming Caregiver Stress

There are several things caregivers can do to manage their stress. Seeking support from friends, family members, or support groups can be helpful. Caregivers should also prioritize taking time for themselves, whether that means going for a walk or spending time with friends. Engaging in regular exercise, maintaining a healthy diet, and getting enough sleep can also aid in managing stress. Furthermore, it is important for caregivers to delegate tasks and ask for help when needed

Results of Overcoming Caregiver Stress

When caregivers are able to manage their stress effectively, it can have significant positive effects on their health and well-being. Caregivers may feel less overwhelmed and more in control of their lives. They may also have more energy and be better able to provide care for their loved ones. Managing stress can also improve relationships with family and friends, and caregivers may find that they are better able to enjoy life outside of their caregiving responsibilities.

How to Handle Caregiver Stress

Handling caregiver stress requires a combination of strategies. Caregivers must prioritize self-care, which includes exercise, healthy eating, and getting enough sleep. It is also important to seek support from friends, family members, or support groups. Caregivers should also consider asking for help when they need it. Taking time for oneself is also important, whether that means going for a walk or spending time with friends. Caregiver stress is a prevalent issue that can have serious consequences for the caregiver. Therefore, caregivers must take steps to manage their stress. This includes seeking support from family and friends, prioritizing self-care, and delegating tasks. By effectively managing their stress, caregivers can improve their health and wellbeing and provide better care for their loved ones.

Frequently Asked Questions: (FAQs)

What causes caregiver stress?

Caregiver stress can be caused by lack of support, isolation, financial strain, and dealing with complex medical issues.

What are the signs of caregiver stress?

Signs of caregiver stress can include difficulty sleeping, lack of energy, feelings of hopelessness, and irritability.

What can caregivers do to manage their stress?

Caregivers can manage their stress by seeking support from friends and family members, prioritizing self-care, and delegating tasks.

What are the effects of caregiver stress?

Long-term stress can lead to serious health problems for the caregiver such as depression, anxiety, high blood pressure, and heart disease.

How can managing stress improve caregivers' lives?

Managing stress can improve caregivers' lives by helping them feel less overwhelmed and more in control of their lives. They may also have more energy and be better able to provide care for their loved ones.

WORRY

For a full-time caregiver, worry can be a constant state of concern, apprehension, or unease related to their caregiving responsibilities. It involves being preoccupied with the well-being, health, safety, and overall quality of life of the person they are caring for. Worry may arise from various factors, such as the physical or emotional health of the care recipient, managing daily tasks and routines, financial or logistical challenges, and the caregiver's own physical and emotional well-being. It can be an ongoing and exhausting aspect of being a full-time caregiver, often requiring support and self-care strategies to manage.

As a full-time caregiver, daily responsibilities can range from cooking and cleaning to administering medication and providing emotional support. While the role of a caregiver can be fulfilling, it can also be emotionally taxing and physically demanding. Full-time caregivers often experience worry, which can have negative effects on their physical and emotional well-being. In this article, we will explore the causes of worry on them, the effects of worry on caregivers, signs of worry, ways to overcome it, and how to handle worry as a full-time caregiver.

"FULL-TIME CAREGIVERS OFTEN EXPERIENCE WORRY."

Causes of Worry in Full-Time Caregivers

Financial Burden: Providing full-time care often means leaving one's job and losing a source of income. This can lead to financial strain and worry about how to make ends meet. Additionally, the cost of healthcare and medication can be overwhelming, especially for those without insurance.

Social Isolation: Full-time caregivers often have limited social interaction outside of their care responsibilities. They may feel isolated from friends and family, resulting in worry about the lack of support and feeling alone in their caregiver role.

Unpredictable Future: Caregivers often face an uncertain future, and this can cause worry. The care receiver's condition may worsen, ultimately leading to the end of their life. This unpredictability can be a source of constant worry and anxiety for the caregiver.

Care Receiver's Condition: The health of the care receiver can be a significant source of worry for full-time caregivers. Caregivers may worry about their loved one's condition worsening, not being able to provide the necessary care, or not being able to meet their loved one's changing needs.

Effects of Worry on Full-Time Caregivers

Physical Effects: Worry can take a toll on a caregiver's physical health. Chronic worry can lead to sleep disturbances, headaches, fatigue, and even digestive problems. Caregivers may also neglect their own health and well-being, leading to greater health problems down the line.

Emotional Effects: Worry can also affect a caregiver's emotional well-being. It can lead to feelings of anxiety, depression, and anger. Caregivers may feel overwhelmed, burned-out and hopeless. Ultimately, these feelings can impact a caregiver's ability to provide quality care to their loved one.

Social Effects: Worry can also lead to social isolation, impacting a caregiver's relationship with family and friends. It may become increasingly difficult to maintain social connections, and as a result, caregivers may withdraw and feel even more isolated.

Signs of Worry in Full-Time Caregivers

Changes in Behavior: Caregivers experiencing worry may display changes in behavior, such as becoming irritable, agitated, or short-tempered. They may also have difficulty concentrating or making decisions.

Physical Symptoms: Chronic worry can also result in physical symptoms, such as headaches, muscle tension, and digestive issues.

Negative Thoughts and Emotions: Caregivers may experience negative thoughts and emotions associated with their role, such as guilt, resentment, and fear.

No More Worrying

Giselle had always been the kind of person who worried about everything. She worried about her job, her health, her relationship with her parents, and even about the weather. However, when her parents started needing more assistance, her worrying began to spiral out of control. She became an extreme worrier, taking her concerns to the extreme.

Giselle lived near Georgetown in Barbados, where she took care of her aging parents, Adela and Tony. Although Adela and Tony were still able to live independently, they required more help with everyday tasks, such as cooking and cleaning. Giselle was happy to provide that help, but it soon became apparent that she was taking on more than she could handle.

Giselle's worrying began to take a toll on her life. She no longer went out, stopped seeing her friends, and gave up the activities she once enjoyed. She even stopped going to the beach, a place she had always loved and frequently visited. As a result, she became isolated and began showing signs of mental fatigue.

One day, while Giselle was cooking dinner, her mother, Adela sat her down to talk. "Giselle," she said, "I've noticed that you've been worrying about everything lately. Is everything okay?"

Giselle sighed. "I don't know, Mom. I'm just worried about you and Dad. What if something happens to one of you? What if I can't take care of you anymore?"

Adela nodded. "I understand, sweetie. But you can't let worrying control your life. You need to take care of yourself, too."

Giselle acknowledged that her mom was correct, but she was unsure how to stop worrying.

One day, as her father was working in the garden, he tripped and fell. Giselle's imagination ran wild, immediately envisioning the worst-case scenario.

"WORRY CAN TAKE A TOLL ON A CAREGIVER'S PHYSICAL HEALTH."

Adela, witnessing her daughter's extreme reaction, realized that something had to change. She gently spoke to Giselle, "Darling, I understand your worry for your father, but you must remember that excessive worrying accomplishes little. It only causes unnecessary stress for yourself and those around you. Maybe it's time to seek some help."

It was then that Giselle realized her worrying accomplished little except making her and those around her miserable.

Giselle took a deep breath and nodded, finally realizing the truth in her mother's words. She discovered a local mental health support group online, and it transformed her life. Through this group, she connected with others who were facing similar struggles, realizing that she wasn't alone.

Additionally, she began seeing a therapist to assist her in effectively coping with her feelings of stress and anxiety.

Over time, she began to feel better. She started going out again, reconnecting with friends, and even going back to the beach. She was excited once again to be able to relax and read some of her favorite novels by R. Lee Moore, Sr.

As life would have it, Giselle met a very handsome and humerous man on the beach after a week. She had noticed him in the distance, but it had been a while since she had been interested in anyone. They struck up a conversation about the weather, and that conversation turned into something more. Roland and Giselle hit it off, and soon, they were spending more and more time together.

For Giselle, it was more than just a new relationship. It was proof that she could overcome her worries and live a happy, fulfilling life.

Today, Giselle is a new person. She's no longer the extreme worrier she once was. She's found love, happiness, and peace of mind. She's still taking care of her parents, but she's doing it in a more balanced way, making time for herself and her own needs.

Through her journey, Giselle realized that worrying accomplishes little except to make her and those around her miserable. She learned that it's okay to ask for help, to take care of herself, and to live life to the fullest. And she hopes that by sharing her story, she can inspire others to do the same.

Overcoming Worry in Full-Time Caregivers
Seeking Support from Family and Friends

It's essential for caregivers to have a support network to assist them navigating the challenges and stress that accompany their role. Friends, family, and other caregivers can offer both emotional and practical support.

Joining Support Groups: Joining a support group can also help caregivers feel less isolated, provide a space to share experiences, and learn coping strategies from others in similar situations.

Practicing Self-care: Caregivers need to take care of their physical and mental well-being. This includes engaging in regular physical activity, practicing mindfulness and relaxation techniques, and ensuring time for self-care and hobbies.

Results Over Time
Improvement in Caregiver's Physical and Mental Health

Making an effort to manage worry and stress can lead to improved physical and mental health for caregivers. This can include better sleep, improved immune function, and better emotional regulation.

"CAREGIVERS SHOULD PRIORITIZE SELF-CARE."

Improved Quality of Care for the Care Receiver

Caregivers who prioritize their well-being are better equipped to provide quality care and emotional support to their loved one.

How to Handle Worry as a Full-Time Caregiver

Recognize and Acknowledge the Worry

The first step in handling worry is recognizing and acknowledging it, rather than trying to ignore it or push it aside.

Find Ways to Cope with Stress

Finding ways to cope with stress is essential in managing worry. This includes practicing relaxation techniques, engaging in regular physical activity, and finding ways to have fun and enjoy life outside of the caregiver role.

Focus on Positive Aspects of Caregiving

Caregiving can be a rewarding and fulfilling experience. Focusing on the positive aspects of the role can help caregivers combat negative emotions and foster a sense of gratitude and purpose.

Finally, as a full-time caregiver, worry can have profound effects on a caregiver's physical, emotional, and social well-being. Recognizing the causes of worry in full-time caregivers and finding ways to overcome it can lead to improved health outcomes for both the caregiver and care receiver. Caregivers should prioritize self-care, seek out social support, and focus on the positive aspects of the caregiver role.

Frequently Asked Questions: (FAQs)

How can I tell if I am an over-worrier?

If you find that you worry excessively about things to the point where it affects your daily life, it may be a sign of being an over-worrier.

How can I seek help for my excessive worrying?

One can seek help through professional therapy, online support groups, or talking to friends and family members.

Is isolation and avoidance common symptoms of excessive worrying?

Yes, for many people, worrying can lead to avoiding or isolating oneself, often due to the fear of the worst-case scenario.

What methods can I use to overcome my worrying habits?

One can overcome worrying habits by challenging negative thoughts, practicing mindfulness meditation, and seeking professional help.

Chapter 3: Breaking the Stigma:
The Importance of Strengthening
Your Mental Health

Good mental health in full-time caregivers refers to a state of well-being where the caregiver is able to effectively manage the physical, emotional, and psychological demands of their caregiving role. This includes being able to cope with stress, maintain a positive outlook, and have a sense of purpose and fulfillment in their caregiving work.

Some indicators of good mental health in full-time caregivers may include:

Resilience: The ability to bounce back from difficult situations and maintain a positive outlook, even in the face of stress and adversity.

Emotional balance: The ability to manage and regulate emotions, such as anger, frustration, and sadness, in a healthy and constructive way.

Self-care: The ability to prioritize self-care activities, such as exercise, relaxation, and socializing, that help maintain physical and mental well-being.

Social support: The presence of a strong social support network, whether it be through friends, family, or support groups, that can provide emotional and practical assistance when needed.

Sense of purpose: A sense of fulfillment and purpose in their caregiving role, with a clear understanding of how their work is making a positive impact on the lives of those they are caring for.

Overall, good mental health in full-time caregivers involves a combination of personal resilience, supportive relationships, and a sense of purpose and fulfillment in their caregiving work.

"MENTAL ILLNESS IS STILL STIGMATIZED IN MANY SOCIETIES."

Why Mental Health Is Essential For Caregivers

Full-time caregivers often provide their loved ones with almost constant care, leaving little time for themselves. Indeed, it is not uncommon for caregivers to neglect their own mental health during this process. Caregiving can be emotionally taxing, and if a caregiver is not prioritizing their mental health, they may find themselves facing burnout, depression and anxiety.

Common Mental Health Struggles for Caregivers

Caregivers are more likely to suffer from depression and anxiety than most other people. They can experience symptoms of trauma such as anxiety, depression, and difficulty sleeping. Studies have also shown that they may have a higher risk of suicide. These issues are largely due to the demands of caregiving alone, and the additional physical and emotional stressors that often come with it, including grief over the loss of the person they are caring for, financial strain, and social isolation.

Why Mental Health Is So Stigmatized Among Caregivers

Mental illness is still stigmatized in many societies, and this stigma is not limited only to professionals. People often assume that because caregivers are providing care and support to their loved ones, they should be able to handle the emotional burden without additional support. This stigma can make caregivers less willing to seek help, which can worsen already established symptoms and potentially delay or prevent treatment.

"GOOD MENTAL HEALTH:
A SENSE OF FULFILLMENT AND PURPOSE IN
OUR CAREGIVING ROLE."

The Benefits of Seeking Mental Health Support

Getting emotional support can help caregivers avoid burnout, depression, and anxiety. It can also assist them in leading a more balanced and fulfilling life as caregivers, reduce the risk of developing depression, and improving overall life satisfaction. Moreover, caregivers can benefit from discussing the challenges they face, identifying their emotions and prioritizing self-care.

How to Prioritize Your Mental Health

The first step in prioritizing mental health is to recognize that it is essential. Caregivers should understand that taking care of themselves is not selfish, but essential for them to continue to provide quality care to their loved ones. Caregivers should set aside time for themselves every day, whether it's taking a walk, reading, or practicing yoga, as this can help them to unwind and relax. Additionally, pursuing a hobby or joining a social group can help to combat social isolation, which can be a significant issue for caregivers.

"CAREGIVERS
SHOULD SET ASIDE TIME
FOR THEMSELVES
EVERY DAY."

Caregivers can also seek professional help from a therapist or support group, which can provide them with a safe environment to process their emotions and share their experiences with others. There are many community organizations that provide support specifically aimed towards caregivers.

As a caregiver, it's essential to recognize that taking care of one's own mental health is not a luxury, but a necessity. Prioritizing your own needs can be challenging, but it is necessary to provide quality care and maintain quality of life. Be kind to yourself, seek support when needed, and stay connected with others. Your own mental health and wellness are just as important as the physical health of the person you're caring for.

Coping with Everyday Challenges: A Mindful Approach to Self-Care

Understanding the Importance of Self-Care

When taking care of another person, it can be easy to forget about your own needs. However, self-care is crucial for full-time caregivers to prevent burnout, maintain good physical and mental health, and provide better care for their loved ones. Self-care can take many forms, including exercise, hobbies, social activities, and relaxation techniques.

Mindful Self-Care Techniques

Incorporating mindfulness into self-care practice can be particularly helpful for full-time caregivers. Mindfulness is the practice of paying attention to the present moment without judgment. This can help caregivers to manage their stress better, stay focused, and preserve their emotional energy.

Mindful breathing is a simple yet effective technique for reducing stress and promoting relaxation. To practice mindful breathing, sit comfortably and focus your attention on your breath. Take deep inhales and exhales, counting to four on the inhale and six on the exhale. Repeat as necessary, and notice the sensations in your body with each breath. Mindful movement is another effective self-care technique for full-time caregivers. Yoga or other gentle exercises can help caregivers release tension, increase flexibility, and reduce stress. Yoga poses like cat-cow, downward dog, and child's pose can be particularly beneficial for caregivers.

"IT IS IMPORTANT FOR CAREGIVERS TO RECOGNIZE THAT SELF-CARE IS NOT A LUXURY."

Other Self-Care Strategies

There are many other self-care strategies that caregivers can utilize to manage everyday challenges. Maintaining a healthy diet and staying hydrated is crucial for physical and mental wellbeing. Getting enough sleep is also important for managing stress and preventing burnout. Engaging in hobbies and activities that bring joy and relaxation can help caregivers to recharge and stay motivated.

Social support is also a critical aspect of self-care for full-time caregivers. Connecting with others who are going through

"CAREGIVERS SHOULD LEARN TO DETACH EMOTIONALLY."

similar experiences can provide emotional validation and reduce feelings of isolation. Joining a caregiver support group or seeking therapy can be helpful for building a support network.

Overcoming Barriers to Self-Care

Despite the many benefits of self-care, it can be challenging for full-time caregivers to make time for themselves. Caregivers may feel guilty or selfish for taking time away from their loved ones, or they may face logistical barriers such as lack of time or resources. It is important for caregivers to recognize that self-care is not a luxury, but a necessity for their own wellbeing and the quality of care they are able to provide.

One approach to overcoming barriers to self-care is to break tasks down into manageable steps. This can involve setting small goals for self-care activities, such as taking a ten minute walk, meditating for five minutes, or scheduling a social outing once a week. Caregivers can also delegate responsibilities to family members or hire respite care to provide them time for self-care.

Self-care is a vital component of the caregiving experience. Mindful self-care techniques, healthy habits, social support, and overcoming barriers can all help caregivers to manage everyday challenges and prevent burnout. By taking care of themselves, caregivers can provide better care for their loved ones and maintain their own wellbeing.

The Guiltless Caregiver - Keeping it Together

At the age of 25, Maria had already experienced more than most people do in a lifetime. She had grown up in a small village in the mountains, where her parents struggled to make ends meet. Her father had died when she was just a child, leaving her mother to raise her and her two younger siblings alone. Despite the challenges, Maria had always been a kind and compassionate person, with a heart full of love and a desire to help others.

After finishing high school, Maria moved to the city to pursue her dream of becoming a nurse. She worked hard to earn her degree and had eventually landed a job at a local hospital. It was there that she met Mrs. Wilson, an elderly woman who had been admitted for treatment of a serious illness.

Maria was immediately drawn to Mrs. Wilson's kind and gentle nature, and the two quickly became close friends. Maria spent hours by Mrs. Wilson's bedside, talking to her and comforting her during the long and often painful days of her treatment.

As Mrs. Wilson's condition worsened, Maria knew that she wanted to do more to help. She began to volunteer her time outside of work, visiting Mrs. Wilson at her home and providing her with the care and attention she needed.

Over time, Maria became Mrs. Wilson's full-time caregiver, dedicating herself to providing the best possible care for her friend. She cooked meals for her, helped her bathe and dress, and provided her with companionship and support.

Despite the long hours and emotional toll of caring for someone who was seriously ill, Maria never complained or showed any signs of resentment. She knew that she was doing something important, something that made a real difference in Mrs. Wilson's life.

As the weeks turned into months, Maria witnessed Mrs. Wilson's health continued to decline. She knew that the end was near, and she prepared herself for the inevitable. When Mrs. Wilson passed away, Maria was devastated. She lost not only a friend but also someone whom she had grown to love like family. However, even in amidst her grief, Maria knew she had done everything in her power to make Mrs. Wilson's final days as comfortable and peaceful as possible.

In the months that followed, Maria continued to pour her heart and soul into caring for others. She volunteered at a hospice, providing care and support to patients who were nearing the end of their lives. She also became involved in her community, organizing events and programs to help those in need.

Throughout it all, Maria remained a kind and compassionate caregiver, never allowing herself to feel guilty or ashamed for the role she played in the lives of those she cared for. She knew she was doing something important, something that made a real difference in the world.

And in the end, that was all that mattered to her.

Emotionally Detaching From Those Around Us

Taking care of others is a noble and often selfless task that requires a great deal of physical, emotional, and mental energy. However, in the midst of all the love and dedication, there may come a time when caregiving causes emotional burnout. Sometimes, caregivers become so overwhelmed by their emotions that they are unable to properly care for others and themselves. One way to deal with this issue is by learning how to detach emotionally when necessary. On this topic, we'll explore the question of whether caregivers should learn to detach emotionally from those we care for and others around us. We'll also discuss how to detach and the best methods for learning this valuable skill.

What is emotional detachment?

Emotional detachment is a coping mechanism that helps individuals disengage from overly emotional situations or people. It can help us avoid becoming overwhelmed or feeling burnt out, and allow us to maintain a level-headed perspective.

Detachment does not mean we completely disconnect or stop caring for others. It is just a simple way to maintain a healthy emotional distance for self-preservation.

Reasons to detach emotionally

Emotional detachment is beneficial in several situations, such as when:

- One needs to cope with overwhelming emotions

- The caregiver needs to take a break from caring for others

- The caregiver has a limited capacity for handling emotional stress

- There is potential danger of developing caregiver burnout

- There are boundary issues between the caregiver and the person being cared for

- Dealing with difficult patients who may be unpleasant or even abusive

Should caregivers detach emotionally?

It is okay for caregivers to detach emotionally from those we care for, as it can be empowering to maintain our boundaries and take care of ourselves. Caregivers have to focus on self-care, too, and that means taking care of their mental and emotional well-being.

However, it is important to note that the level of detachment should always be appropriate for the situation, keeping in mind that some levels of attachment are necessary for effective caregiving.

"SET BOUNDARIES."

How to detach emotionally

Here are some tips on how caregivers can learn to detach emotionally when necessary:

Set boundaries: Establish clear boundaries to prevent being overwhelmed or stretched too thin. Boundaries can serve as a safeguard against stress, negativity, and burnout.

Develop a support system: Seek out those who understand the challenges of caregiving and can offer support and guidance.

Take time for oneself: It's important to take breaks and invest in activities that promote relaxation and mindfulness.

Practice mindfulness: Mindfulness is one of the best self-care practices that can help individuals detach from volatile emotions and reactions.

Practice positive self-talk: Positive self-talk helps to shift attention away from negative thoughts and emotions, and fosters a stronger emotional and mental resilience.

Benefits of emotional detachment

Emotional detachment has several benefits, including:

- It helps to reduce stress and burnout

- It fosters emotional and mental strength

- It helps create healthy boundaries between caregivers and patients- It helps to reduce stress and burnout

- It increases the caregiver's control over their emotions and enhances their overall well-being.

Risks of emotional detachment

Like any coping mechanism, emotional detachment can have consequences if don't strike a healthy balance. If you detach too much, there's a risk of becoming too emotionally disconnected from those around you. This kind of detachment can lead to apathy and disconnection, which can damage relationships and interpersonal connections.

Balancing emotional detachment and attachment

Emotional detachment is not an all-or-nothing approach for caregivers. It's important to find the right balance between emotional attachment and detachment. It's healthy for caregivers to acknowledge their emotions, but they should also learn when and how to release these emotions in a healthy way.

Furthermore, caregiving is essential work, but it becomes a nearly impossible task when a caregiver's emotions become overwhelming. Learning how to emotionally detach can benefit a caregiver in several ways, allowing them to maintain healthy boundaries and avoid burnout.

However, it's important to remember that emotional detachment is not the only solution. Striking the right balance between attachment and detachment is crucial to ensure healthy relationships with those we care for.

Frequently Asked Questions: (FAQs)

Is it normal to have difficulty detaching emotionally from my relatives or patients as a caregiver?

Yes, it's normal. Caregivers often experience a range of emotions when caring for others, including empathy, stress, and overwhelm. However, developing emotional detachment can help maintain relationships while taking care of yourself.

How can I tell if I'm emotionally detached from those I care for?

If you find yourself feeling nothing for those you care for or feel disconnected from them, you may be experiencing emotional detachment. However, it's important to distinguish emotional detachment from burnout, which can cause similar symptoms.

Can emotional detachment be harmful for caregivers or the cared-for?

If emotional detachment is taken too far, it can become harmful, and ultimately damaging to relationships. Emotional detachment should be balanced and appropriate for the situation and should not be used as an excuse for neglect or unkindness.

Are there any other ways to cope with caregiver burnout?

Yes, other ways to cope with caregiver burnout include self-care, practicing stress reduction techniques like meditation, exercise, and setting achievable goals. Seeking out support groups or a therapist can also help caregivers dealing with burnout.

"POSITIVE SELF-TALK HELPS TO SHIFT ATTENTION AWAY FROM NEGATIVE THOUGHTS."

Stress, Worry and Anxiety - Are They All The Same?

Worry, stress, and anxiety are some of the most common emotions that people face in their daily lives. While these three terms are often used interchangeably, they differ from each other in several ways.

Worry occurs in your mind. Stress happens in your body. Anxiety, on the other hand, affects both the mind and the body. Stress is the body's response to a threat, whereas anxiety is the body's reaction to the stress.

Worry tends to be more centered on thoughts in our mind, whereas, anxiety is more deeply rooted and felt throughout our bodies.

Understanding Worry

Worry is a feeling of unease or concern about something that may happen in the future. It is a common emotion that everyone experiences at some point in their lives. Worrying can be a normal and healthy response to a stressful situation. For example, if you have an upcoming exam, it's natural to worry about how you will perform. However, when worry becomes excessive and turns into chronic worrying, it can have negative consequences on your mental and physical health.

Why Do We Worry?
People worry for various reasons, including:
- Fear of the unknown
- Concern for the future
- Pressures from work or family
- Lack of control over a situation
- Negative thinking patterns

Effects of Worry on the Mind and Body

Worry can have several effects on both our minds and bodies. **Some of the common effects include:**

- Difficulty concentrating
- Insomnia
- Increased irritability and agitation
- Muscle tension and aches
- Headaches
- Fatigue

Understanding Stress

Stress is a physical response to a perceived threat or challenge. It is a natural and healthy response that prepares our bodies to take action and stay safe. However, when stress becomes chronic, it can have negative consequences on our mental and physical health.

Effects of Stress on the Mind and Body

Stress can have several effects on both our minds and bodies. Some of the common effects include:

- Anxiety
- Depression
- Headaches
- High blood pressure
- Heart disease
- Digestive problems
- Insomnia
- Fatigue

"WORRY, STRESS, AND ANXIETY ARE THREE DISTINCT EMOTIONS."

Understanding Anxiety

Anxiety is a feeling of fear or apprehension about a future event or situation. It is a normal and healthy emotion that everyone experiences at some point in their lives. However, when anxiety becomes chronic, it can have negative consequences on our mental and physical health.

Types of Anxiety Disorders

There are several types of anxiety disorders, including:

Generalized Anxiety Disorder: This type of anxiety disorder is characterized by excessive worry about everyday situations.

Panic Disorder: This type of anxiety disorder is characterized by sudden and unexpected panic attacks.

Social Anxiety Disorder: This type of anxiety disorder is characterized by excessive fear of social situations.

Obsessive-Compulsive Disorder (OCD): This type of anxiety disorder is characterized by obsessive thoughts and compulsive behaviors.

Post-Traumatic Stress Disorder (PTSD): This type of anxiety disorder is caused by a traumatic event such as war, natural disaster, or physical abuse.

Effects of Anxiety on the Mind and Body

Anxiety can have several effects on both our minds and bodies. **Some of the common effects include:**

- Muscle tension
- Fatigue
- Insomnia
- Panic attacks
- Digestive problems
- Headaches
- Sweating
- Increased heart rate

Worry, stress, and anxiety are three distinct emotions that can have a significant impact on our mental and physical health. By understanding the differences between these emotions and learning how to manage them, we can lead happier and healthier lives. Seeking help from a mental health professional is always the best option if you are struggling with any of these emotions.

"ANXIETY CAN HAVE SEVERAL EFFECTS ON BOTH OUR MINDS AND BODIES."

Frequently Asked Questions: (FAQs)

Is anxiety the same as stress?

No, anxiety is not the same as stress. While both anxiety and stress can cause physical and emotional symptoms, anxiety is a feeling of fear or apprehension about a future event or situation, while stress is a physical response to a perceived threat or challenge.

Can worrying cause anxiety?

Yes, chronic worrying can lead to anxiety. When you worry excessively, you activate your body's stress response, which can lead to physical and emotional symptoms of anxiety.

What are the long-term effects of stress?

If left untreated, chronic stress can lead to several long-term effects such as high blood pressure, heart disease, and a weakened immune system.

How can I manage stress and anxiety?

Managing stress and anxiety involves several strategies, including:
- *Exercise*
- *Mindfulness meditation*
- *Deep breathing exercises*
- *Getting enough sleep*
- *Eating a healthy diet*
- *Seeking support from friends and family*
- *Seeking help from a mental health professional*

"HUMOR IS A GREAT STRESS BUSTER."

Humor and Mental Health
How important is humor for a full-time caregiver?

As a full-time caregiver, the job can be tough, overwhelming and stressful. It is unlike any other job, as it requires not only a lot of physical demands but also emotional and mental ones. With all of these demands, it is crucial to find ways to relieve that built-up stress and tension, and one of the best ways to do so is through humor. Humor has been found to be an effective coping mechanism when dealing with stressful situations. It is important to incorporate humor in your life as a caregiver, and this topic explores why, the benefits of humor, and examples of humor.

The benefits of using humor in caregiving

Humor can be a powerful tool for caregivers to help them cope with the daily demands of their job. It's an excellent way to cope with the daily demands and stress. Also it can help you deal with both physical and emotional pains well as relax, lift your mood, and boost your overall energy levels.

The following are some of the benefits of humor in caregiving:

Stress reduction

Humor is a great stress buster. It helps to reduce tension, improve mood, and lower stress levels. Laughter has been found to decrease the production of stress hormones such as cortisol and adrenaline, which helps to reduce the physical symptoms of stress, such as high blood pressure, headaches, and muscle tension.

Improve Mental Health

Humor can help to improve mental health by reducing depression and anxiety. Laughter prompts the release of endorphins, which are natural mood-enhancing chemicals in the body. It can also help with feelings of isolation and loneliness, which can lead to depression.

Fosters Positivity

A positive mind-set is crucial in caregiving. By incorporating humor into your life, you can help to shift your mind-set from negative to positive. Humor can help you see the bright side of things, even in tough situations, and help you maintain a positive attitude towards caregiving responsibilities.

Examples of humor incorporated into caregiving:

The following are examples of how humor can be incorporated into caregiving:

Jokes and humorous stories: Telling jokes or sharing humorous stories with those you care for can help brighten their day. It can also help to relieve their stress and worries, making them feel more relaxed and comfortable.

Gentle teasing: Gentle teasing can be an effective way to lighten the mood and help those you care for feel more comfortable. It can help build a deeper connection with them and show them that you genuinely care for them.

Have a daily laugh: Start your day with laughter. You can watch a funny video, tell a joke, or listen to a funny podcast. Laughter is the best medicine, and it can help you deal with the stress of caregiving.

Tell funny stories: Tell funny stories about your life or the life of the person you are caring for. You can share stories about an embarrassing moment, a funny experience, or a humorous mistake. This can help you both relax and laugh together.

Use humor in your communication

Use humor in your communication with the person you are caring for. You can use funny voices, puns, or jokes to make them laugh. This can make your communication more engaging and enjoyable for both of you.

Watch humorous videos

Watch humorous videos together with the person you are caring for. You can enjoy funny animal videos, comedy shows, or viral videos. This can bring laughter and strengthen your connection.

As a full-time caregiver, it is easy to forget about taking care of yourself. Humor is an effective way to reduce stress, boost your mood, and take care of your mental and emotional health. The benefits of incorporating humor into your caregiving routine are many, and there are many different ways to do so. By using humor, you can create a more positive overall experience for both yourself and those you care for.

Here are some jokes about caregiving that can bring a little light to the situation.

"Caregiving is like riding a roller coaster, except there's no thrill, and you're always on the ride."

"If you think caring for a toddler is tough, try caring for an adult who acts like one."

"Caregiving is like a box of chocolates: you never know what you are going to get."

"Caregiving is not for the faint-hearted. It's for those who have a big heart."

"If you think caregiving is easy, try doing it without caffeine."

"The only time I get a break from caregiving is when I am asleep, and even that is not guaranteed."

Being a caregiver is an act of love and dedication that demands a lot of patience, strength, and compassion. But it doesn't always have to be a tedious job. Using funny sayings and humor in your caregiving routine can bring a lot of positive changes and lighten up the mood. Remember to have a sense of humor to make the job much more manageable.

Frequently Asked Questions: (FAQs)

What are the benefits of adding humor to caregiving?

The benefits of adding humor to caregiving include stress relief, improved communication, and a stronger relationship between the caregiver and the recipient.

How can comedy shows be helpful in caregiving?

Watching a funny comedy show or a movie can be an excellent way to relieve stress. Laughter is contagious and can help you forget your troubles and put you in a good mood.

Is gentle teasing a good way to incorporate humor in caregiving?

Yes, gentle teasing can be an effective way to lighten the mood and help those you care for feel more comfortable. It can help build a deeper connection with them, and show them that you genuinely care for them.

Can humor be inappropriate when caring for someone?

Yes, humor can be inappropriate, especially if it is hurtful or insensitive. It is essential to use humor carefully and make sure it doesn't offend anyone.

Chapter 4: Finding Strength in Community:

Building a Support Network for Caregivers

A support network for caregivers is a group of people who provide emotional, practical, and/or financial support to caregivers. This network may include family members, friends, neighbors, healthcare professionals, and support groups. Building a support network can help caregivers feel less isolated, reduce stress, and improve the quality of life for both the caregiver and the person receiving care.

Identifying Potential Sources of Support

The first step in building a support network as a caregiver is to identify potential sources of support. This can include family members, friends, neighbors, religious organizations, community centers, and support groups. It's important to reach out to people who you trust and who can provide the type of support you need, whether it's emotional, practical, or financial.

Joining a Support Group

One of the most effective ways to build a support network as a caregiver is to join a support group. Support groups allow caregivers to connect with others who are going through similar experiences, share their struggles and successes, and access valuable resources and information. Support groups can be found through local hospitals, community centers, and online forums.

Building Connections with Other Caregivers

Building connections with other caregivers is also an essential part of building a support network. Caregivers can attend local events, meet ups, and support group meetings to connect with others, share their experiences, and build relationships. It's important to listen to other caregivers and learn from their

"IT'S IMPORTANT TO REACH OUT TO PEOPLE WHO YOU TRUST."

experiences, as well as share your own. This can help you feel less alone and more supported, as well as provide valuable insights and advice.

Building Relationships with Family and Friends

Caregiving for family can become a source for support as well as a source of distress. When relationships are strained or uncomfortable, caregiving for that person will take patience and wisdom to get through it. Keep in mind that you are not alone.

Caregivers can feel alone and abandoned at times. Learn to share your situation with those you trust will care. Building relationships with family and friends can be an important part of building a support network as a caregiver. It's important to be open and honest with loved ones about your experience as a

"BUILDING A NETWORK
OF SUPPORT IS ESSENTIAL."

caregiver, and to let them know what type of support you need. This can include help with household tasks, providing respite care, or simply being there to listen and provide emotional support.

Accessing Community Resources

Accessing community resources can also be an important part of building a support network as a caregiver. Local, state, and federal organizations often provide a range of programs and services designed to support caregivers, including respite care, counseling services, educational resources, and financial assistance. It's important to research these resources and take advantage of any that may be available to you.

Becoming an Advocate for Caregivers

Finally, caregivers can also become advocates for themselves and others by speaking out about their experiences and raising awareness about the challenges of caregiving. This can include participating in local and national caregiver organizations, speaking to lawmakers, and sharing their stories with the media. By advocating for themselves and others, caregivers can help create a more supportive and understanding community for all those who provide care for their loved ones.

Building a network of support is essential for caregivers, and finding strength in community is an excellent way to overcome the challenges of caregiving. By identifying potential sources of support, joining a support group, building connections with other caregivers, building relationships with family and friends, accessing community resources, and becoming an advocate for other caregivers, caregivers can build a strong and supportive network that can help them navigate the challenges of caregiving and maintain their own physical and emotional well-being.

Frequently Asked Questions: (FAQs)

What makes emotional support essential when building a support network for full-time caregivers?

Emotional support provides a listening ear and empathy to help caregivers reduce stress and burnout.

What benefits can in-person support groups offer to full-time caregivers compared to online support groups?

In-person support groups may provide more tangible emotional support since the group members meet face-to-face and can form deeper connections.

How can support groups for full-time caregivers help them to better handle stress?

Support groups offer a safe space for caregivers to share their experiences and receive advice on how to manage stress.

What strategies can a full-time caregiver utilize to maintain a strong support network?

Maintaining a strong network involves regular check-ins, updates, and expressions of gratitude to support group members.

How can caregivers address possible conflicts within their support groups?

Open communication, active listening, and compassion are essential for addressing conflicts within support groups.

Chapter 5: When Caregiving Ends:

How to Transition to a New Life as a Former Full-Time Caregiver

When caring for a loved one who is ill or aging, it is a natural instinct to focus on their needs and wellbeing. However, it is important to remember that caregiving comes with a definitive end. Eventually, the care recipient will pass away or transition to a long-term care facility. Preparing for this end can be challenging, but it is an essential part of the caregiving journey. We'll discuss how to smoothly transition from a caregiver to a free person again and suggest some things to consider and steps to take.

Understanding the End-of-Life Process

One of the most critical aspects of preparing for the end of caregiving is understanding the end-of-life process. Often, caregivers and their loved ones avoid discussing death and what to expect during this time. However, having an honest and open conversation about death and the dying process can be beneficial for all involved.

For instance, discussing the type of care the care recipient would like towards the end of their life helps ensure their wishes are respected. It also helps in preparing the caregiver emotionally, mentally, and practically.

"PREPARING TO TRANSITION CAN BE OVERWHELMING."

The Emotions of Ending Caregiving

Caregiving can be a fulfilling experience that turns into an intimate connection between the caregiver and the patient. Losing that connection can bring a variety of emotions. Many caregivers report feeling a sense of loss or grief, disorientation, or even guilt that they are feeling relief. These are all normal emotions that you may experience during this time of transition. You don't have to go through them alone.

The First Steps

One of the most practical steps is to set up a support system before caregiving ends. Preparing to transition can be overwhelming, and having someone to rely on can ease the burden. Talk to your support network about what you currently need and how they can help. It may be helpful to seek counseling to navigate the complex emotional landscape.

Things to Consider

Remember that your identity as a caregiver doesn't define you. You have unique skills and qualities that can be channeled into other areas of your life beyond caregiving. Take some time to assess what matters to you- are there any passions or hobbies that you had to put on hold during caregiving? Focus on returning to those pursuits and building a new life and routine beyond caregiving.

Coping with Insensitive Suggestions

It is difficult to overstate the importance of having a supportive network. However, there are times when loved ones, family members, or friends may offer insensitive advice or suggestions.

Regrettably, some of these suggestions can go so far as to blame you for becoming a caregiver in the first place or undermine your experience of caring for another person. It is important to remember that these individuals may not fully comprehend the emotional and physical effort involved in caregiving.

Taking Care of Yourself

Caregiving is a demanding job that can take a toll on the caregiver's physical and emotional health. As the end of caregiving approaches, it is even more critical to prioritize self-care.

Taking the time to exercise, eat healthily, and get enough sleep can help caregivers maintain their physical health. It is also essential to take breaks and engage in enjoyable activities to prevent emotional exhaustion and burnout.

Managing Practical Matters

In addition to taking care of themselves emotionally and physically, caregivers must also consider the practicalities that come with the end of caregiving. For many caregivers, the end of full-time care brings changes to their financial situation. It may be worthwhile to consult with a financial advisor or lawyer to ensure you are taking advantage of everything your loved one is eligible for during end-of-life planning. Make sure everything is organized and that you know what steps to take.

Additionally, caregivers may need to prepare the care recipient's home for sale or consider assisted living options. Taking care of these practical matters well in advance can help to alleviate stress and prevent last-minute decisions.

Practicing Self-Compassion

Finally, practicing self-compassion is a crucial component of preparing for the end of caregiving. Caregivers often feel a sense of guilt or a lack of fulfillment as their role comes to an end. It is essential to recognize that these feelings are normal and that caregivers should practice self-compassion rather than judgement.

This may mean embracing the emotions that come with closure, focusing on the positive memories and moments shared with the care recipient, and finding new ways to give back to the community.

Tips for a Smooth Transition

- Take Baby Steps: Give yourself time to adjust, this can be a massive adjustment for you.

- Don't be too hard on Yourself: You did the best you could to help your loved one. Don't regret things you couldn't do.

- Take Care of Yourself: It's essential to take this time to focus on your health: visit your doctor, eat well, exercise, and find mental clarity doing activities you enjoy.

- Seek Out Your Interests: Reconnect with friends, or find local groups that match your interests.

- Volunteer: You can volunteer with seniors or volunteer with animals or a cause that you feel passionate about.

Conclusion

As your caregiving journey comes to an end, it can be challenging to know where to begin preparing for this transition. However, understanding the end-of-life process, creating a support system, taking care of oneself, managing practical matters, and practicing self-compassion can help to mitigate stress, prevent burnout, and prepare for the end of caregiving. Remembering to take care of oneself, both physically and emotionally, is crucial during this challenging time.

We trust that this has shed light on the hidden emotions and struggles of full-time caregivers. Throughout the five chapters, we have explored the emotional turmoil that caregivers face, the stigma around prioritizing their mental health, and the challenges they encounter on a daily basis.

We have also learned about the importance of practicing self-care and the benefits of building a strong support network. It's crucial to recognize and acknowledge the significant role played by caregivers in our society, both in terms of their personal sacrifice and the impact they have on their loved ones' lives. The insights shared in this info novel will help empower caregivers to address their emotional difficulties and prioritize their mental health.

We hope that the information provided will serve as a resource for caregivers to implement a mindful approach to self-care and build supportive communities. By doing so, caregivers can improve their well-being and provide even better care to their loved ones. Ultimately, it's our hope that this book will contribute to a healthier, more supportive society for caregivers.

Frequently Asked Questions: (FAQs)

How long will it take to transition from a life of caregiving to a new routine?

While every situation is different, it is common for caregivers to take several months or even a year to transition smoothly.

How do I deal with the guilt of feeling relieved that my caregiving responsibilities have ended?

It is natural to experience some relief that your caregiving journey has ended, but it is also common to feel guilty about it. Speaking with a counselor or someone in your support network can help you process those emotions.

Who should I consult with if caregiving has financially impacted me?

Consulting with a financial advisor or a lawyer is an excellent step to help understand your unique financial situation and any benefits you or your loved one are entitled to.

How do I cope with insensitive suggestions from family and friends who have never been caregivers?

Remember that those individuals may not have a full understanding of what you've gone through. Focusing on your support network and what works best for you can help you find stability in times of emotional stress.

How do I start reconnecting with my passions or hobbies after caregiving ends?

Taking small steps, such as contacting old friends, diving into hobbies, and volunteering, can help reignite your passions and interests and find meaning outside of caregiving.

References

Page iv - Dedication: How Many Caregivers in the U.S.?
https://www.caregiver.org/resource/caregiver-statistics-demographics/

Page ix - A Caregiver Defined:
https://en.wikipedia.org/wiki/Caregiver

Page 13 - Finding Support and Resources
https://www.autismsociety.org

Page 160 - Stress, Worry and Anxiety - Are They All The Same?
https://www.stress.org/the-difference-between-worry-stress-and-anxiety
https://www.medicalnewstoday.com/articles/stress-vs-anxiety
https://www.psychologytoday.com/intl/blog/the-squeaky-wheel/201603/10-crucial-differences-between-worry-and-anxiety

Other Resources:
Definitons and content of the 15 emotions discussed are from various resource websites including:
https://www.merriam-webster.com/
https://www.caregiver.org/,
https://www.helpguide.org/,
https://www.aarp.org/caregiving/,
https://www.rootsofloneliness.com/

Books by R. Lee Moore, Sr.

Think FEEL SPEAK *Write* **Do**

A Guide to Fulfilling Your Purpose

www.thinkfeelspeakwritedo.com

Coming soon!

A Caregiver's Guide to OVERCOMING...

Explore effective steps for caregivers to overcome common emotions experienced, from **anger, depression,** and **guilt** to **lonelines** and **stress.** Concise, informative and easy reading; five book series.

A Guiltless Caregiver's Resource.

Contact R. Lee Moore, Sr.

For Book Signings & Speaking Engagements:

Email: RLeeMooreSr@gmail.com

Phone: (844) 246-2200

Website: www.**Moore**BooksR.us

Mail: R. Lee Moore, Sr.
                295 E. Swedesford Road, #288
                Wayne, PA 19087

www.ingramcontent.com/pod-product-compliance
Lightning Source LLC
Chambersburg PA
CBHW051151120626
46547CB00012B/1041